HOW [...] MA[...] NEXT GENERATION!

POCKET SIZED!

presented by
BEN DUNN
with
FRED PERRY
ROD ESPINOSA
JOE WIGHT
and
DAVID HUTCHISON

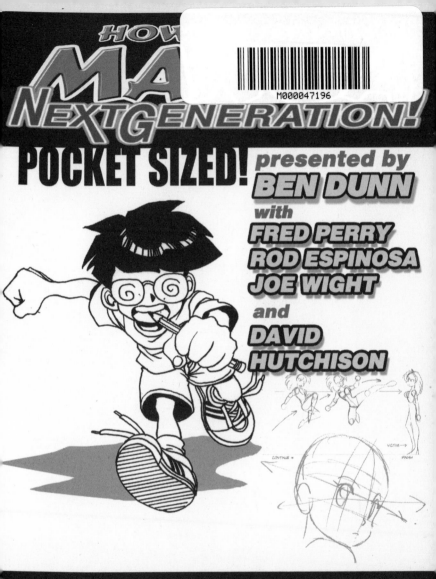

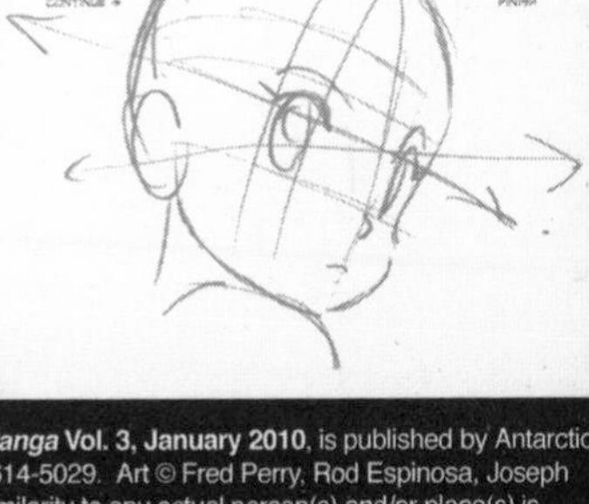

Antarctic Press Presents: How to Draw Manga Next Generation Pocket Manga Vol. 3, January 2010, is published by Antarctic Press, 7272 Wurzbach, Suite #204, San Antonio, Texas, 78240. FAX#: (210) 614-5029.
Printed and bound in Canada by Impremerie Lebonfon, Inc.

HOW TO DRAW MANGA!

WARDROBE PRIMER!

:WITH BEN DUNN.

HOW TO DRAW MANGA!

WARDROBE PRIMER!

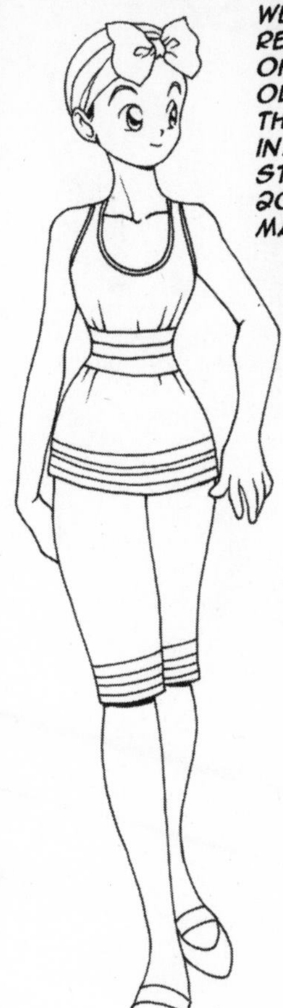

WARDROBE IS EVERYTHING! WITHOUT IT, WE'D BE WEARING NOTHING! CHARACTERS' WARDROBE REFLECTS MANY ASPECTS ABOUT WHAT TYPE OF PEOPLE THEY ARE. MOST IMPORTANTLY, THE OUTFITS WORN BY YOUR CHARACTERS WILL TELL THE READER WHAT ERA YOUR CHARACTERS RESIDE IN. FOR EXAMPLE, IF YOU WERE TO ILLUSTRATE A STORY THAT TOOK PLACE AT THE TURN OF THE 20TH CENTURY, THERE WOULD DEFINITELY BE MANY DRASTIC FASHION DIFFERENCES.

TO THE LEFT, WE HAVE A GIRL IN SWIMWEAR. BIKINIS WEREN'T INVENTED AS OF THE DATE OF OUR STORY...SO HAVING HER IN ONE WOULD TAKE AWAY THE BELIEVABILITY OF HER RESIDING IN THE EARLY 1900S...EVEN THE SWIMSUIT I DREW HERE IS VERY RISQUE FOR THE TIME!

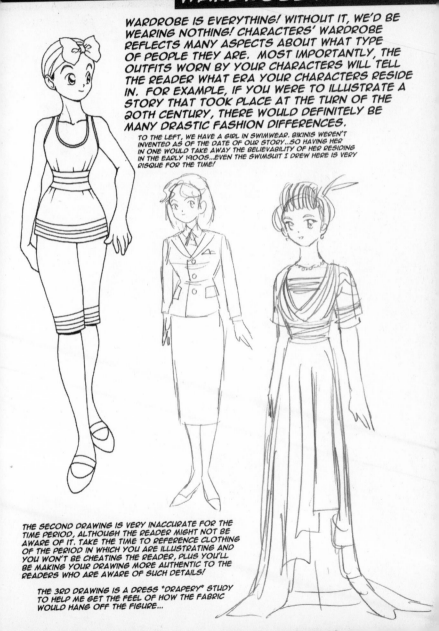

THE SECOND DRAWING IS VERY INACCURATE FOR THE TIME PERIOD, ALTHOUGH THE READER MIGHT NOT BE AWARE OF IT. TAKE THE TIME TO REFERENCE CLOTHING OF THE PERIOD IN WHICH YOU ARE ILLUSTRATING AND YOU WON'T BE CHEATING THE READER, PLUS YOU'LL BE MAKING YOUR DRAWING MORE AUTHENTIC TO THE READERS WHO ARE AWARE OF SUCH DETAILS!

THE 3RD DRAWING IS A DRESS "DRAPERY" STUDY TO HELP ME GET THE FEEL OF HOW THE FABRIC WOULD HANG OFF THE FIGURE...

HOW TO DRAW MANGA!
WARDROBE PRIMER!

DETAILS!

A LOT OF THE HIGH FASHION OR "HAUTE COUTURE" OF THE EARLY 1900'S HAD A GREAT DEGREE OF DETAIL AND ORNATENESS. ILLUSTRATING THESE DETAILS WILL GIVE YOUR DRAWINGS EVEN GREATER RICHNESS AND BELIEVABILITY.

HOW TO DRAW MANGA!
WARDROBE PRIMER!

REFERENCE!

WHEN DRAWING FASHIONS FROM A CERTAIN PERIOD, IT IS CRUCIAL THAT YOU FIND GOOD REFERENCE MATERIAL IN REGARDS TO IT. ONLY THEN WILL YOUR WARDROBES HAVE THE LOOK OF AUTHENTICITY THAT YOU'RE GOING FOR. THE KEY IS TO PUT YOUR CHARACTERS IN THE ENVIRONMENT THAT SURROUNDS THEM AND NOT TO CONTRADICT THAT WITH WARDOBE THAT IS ENTIRELY OUT OF PLACE FOR THAT ERA...UNLESS YOUR CHARACTERS ARE TIME-TRAVELLERS!

Day Wear 1900–1902

THE MORE YOU REFERENCE AND STUDY A PARTICULAR SUBJECT, THE BETTER UNDERSTANDING YOU'LL HAVE OF THE SUBJECT, AND THEN YOU CAN TAKE SOME CREATIVE LIBERTIES AND DESIGN THINGS IN ACCORDANCE TO THOSE PRINCIPLES.

PRACTICE PAGE

1 THE BIG HEAD SHOT

Comments:
This type of cover is typically used to showcase strong emotion and to show people how well you can draw heads. Most of the time I find the "big head" shot is used when the artist is in a hurry to meet a deadline, though if done very well, it can be very impressive. I don't like using it too often, as it can be very boring layout-wise and it's too easy in many cases.
I used a large head shot for *Ninja High School* #81 because I wanted to show just what a badass Dog Supreme was without giving away the story inside. The trickle of blood from his nose was added to give the reader pause and make him ask, "What caused that?"

ADVANTAGES:
1. Easy to do in a pinch.
2. Conveys very strong emotions.
3. Easily attracts attention from a distance.
4. Simple layout.
5. A variation of this is known as "the multiple head shot." This is when many heads are used in a cover. (See *Silver Cross* #3 for example).

DISADVANTAGES:
1. Boring at times.

HOW TO DRAW MANGA: DESIGNING COVER ELEMENTS

2 THE LARGE-SCALE ACTION SEQUENCE

Comments:
One of the most exciting types of cover you can do is the large action sequence. Usually it is a part of the story that the cover artist finds particulary exciting. It is one of the most effective ways to tell the reader that there is something really cool going on inside this comic and that they must pick it up to find out what the comic is all about.
On this cover of *Mighty Tiny* #5 I opted to show the massive airship battle but juxtaposed the two main characters to show the how small they are in comparison to the events taking place. Large-scale sequences like this are very effective almost all the time and they are a lot of fun to do, but they are very time-consuming and can be difficult to lay out just right.

ADVANTAGES:
1. Always exciting and colorful.
2. Tell the story with one image.

DISADVANTAGES:
1. TIme-consuming.
2. Always a danger of giving away too much.
3. Difficult to lay out effectively.

3 THE SMALL-SCALE ACTION SEQUENCE

Comments:
Basically the same as the large-scale version, but instead focuses mostly on characters reacting to their surroundings or recreating a part of the story. A great way to show many characters at once doing all sorts of things. Can be very colorful and exciting if done well. A slight variation of this theme is the "multiple standing around sequence," when many characters are simply just standing. I usually avoid these, as they can get boring pretty fast.
The cover of *Ninja High School Yearbook* #13 shows most of the main *NHS V.2* characters running around. This allowed me to showcase them in one fell swoop and hopefully get the reader interested enough to pick up the book based solely on what the characters were doing.

ADVANTAGES:
1. Showcase many characters at once.
2. Keeps the action personal.

DISADVANTAGES:
1. Can appear too crowded.
2. Difficult to lay out.

4 THE LONE FIGURE

Comments:
Certainly one of the best types of cover to employ is the lone figure shot. Elegent and direct, it tells the reader, "I am the focus of this story!" It also allows the artist to really get into the character and make that character really stand out. It's also a way for the artist to showcase his ability to draw the figure. It's often recommended to use a character who fits the mood of the story, though it can be used simply to show what the character can do. A static character usually portrays confidence, power, or high emotion. A character in action usually portrays ability and movement.
In this cover to *Ninja High School* #86, the figure is standing confident as a fleet of battleships moves overhead. By doing this, I show her as the unquestioned ruler of all she surveys!

ADVANTAGES:
1. Simple layout, but very effective.
2. Directly tells the reader who the main focus is on.

DISADVANTAGES:
1. Can be overused.

5 THE CENTER FIGURE TRIUMPH SHOT

Comments:
This type of cover is typically used to entice the reader with an "Oh, no!" reaction. Whenever a shot is used that shows the "bad guy" seemingly triumphant over the "good guy," that can't be good news. Effective in its ability to get the curious reader, it is for the most part a cliché in comics, because we all know the good guys will triumph in the end. However, it is fun to do, and believe it or not, still works on a basic level.
This cover of *Zetraman: Revival* #1 was used because I felt the need show the old-fashionedess of the story. Also, since it dealt with a new origin of the Zetramen, it conveyed a sense of "out with the old and in with the new."

ADVANTAGES:
1. Still works and conveys a sense of nostalgia.
2. Simple layout.

DISADVANTAGES:
1. Can only be used sparingly.

6 THE MULTI-CHARACTER COLLAGE

Comments:
This type of cover is typically used to show a lot of characters, usually with 1-3 individuals as the main focus. Simple layout-wise and effective as a way of showing the readers the varied cast, this type of cover is often used for a first issue or anniversary issue.
This cover for the color version of *Ninja High School* #1 was used in order to show the entire cast of the book in one fell swoop.

ADVANTAGES:
1. Shows the entire cast at once.
2. Simple layout.

DISADVANTAGES:
1. TIme-consuming if cast is complicated.
2. Cannot be used that often.

HOW TO DRAW MANGA:
DOING A COVER: START TO FINISH

1: LAYOUT AND DESIGN

Okay, here we go.

I've just plotted out the issue of *Ninja High School* #90 and I need to do a cover.

The first step is to decide what kind of cover I want. Since it is the start of a new storyline, I opt for the multi-character collage but limit it to 3 characters—Tomorrow Girl, Warrior Nun Areala and Ramen Rider—because I don't want to reveal too many secrets of the story.

Get some scratch paper and start sketching a layout. You will sometimes go through many such layouts before you become satisfied with one, or you may just have to do 1 or 2 if you are a seasoned pro like I am.

I find the first layout makes Tomorrow Girl look too confrontational and cuts across Ramen Rider. So I opt to have TM have her arm on her chest and give her a more innocent look.

Once you have decided on the layout, you go to the pencil stage.

LAYOUT 1

LAYOUT 2

2: ROUGH PENCIL STAGE

At this stage, you start pencilling the final version of your cover.

HOW TO DRAW MANGA:
DOING A COVER: START TO FINISH
3: FINAL PENCILLING STAGE AND INKING

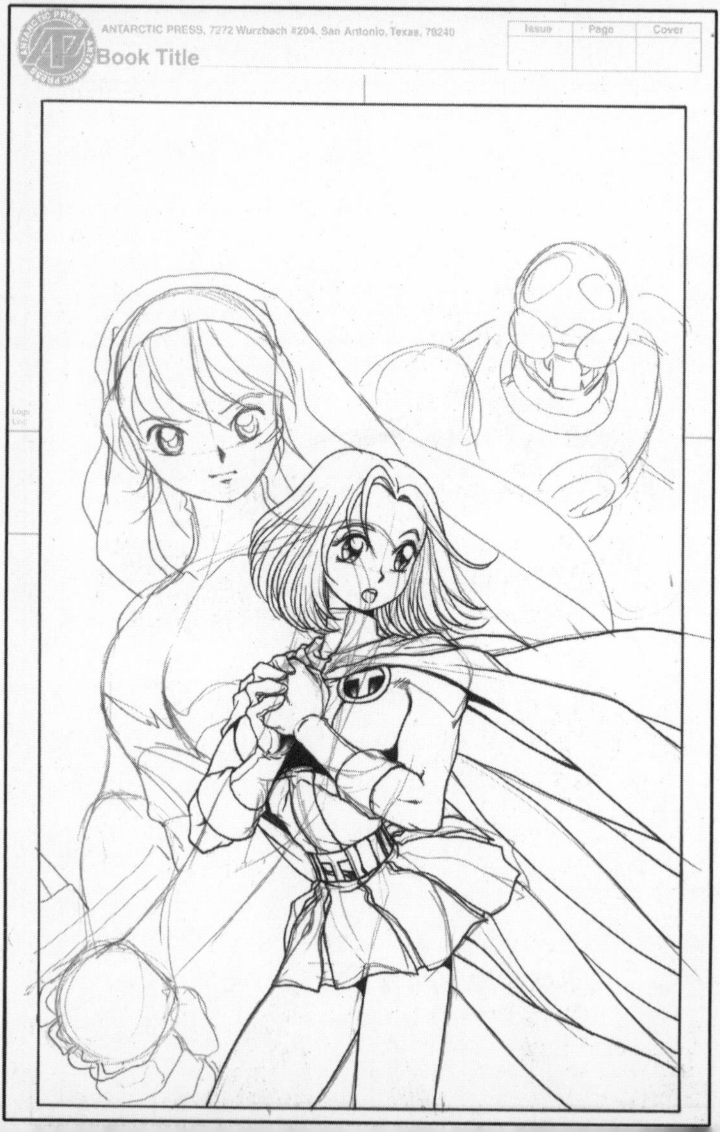

HOW TO DRAW MANGA: DOING A COVER: START TO FINISH

At this stage, I make a change in the story—Ramen Rider is dropped and Little Hu is included. I erase Ramen Rider and insert Little Hu.

DOING A COVER: START TO FINISH

Now all the characters are inked. I don't do a background, opting to let the colorist fill in the space. Once you are done inking, erase the pencils.

HOW TO DRAW MANGA:
DOING A COVER: START TO FINISH

THE FINISHED COVER! READY TO BE SCANNED AND COLORED!

PRACTICE PAGE

HOW TO DRAW MANGA: THE FRED PERRY WAY

CHARACTER DESIGN

HEY! I'M BACK TO SHOW YOU SOME MORE TECHNIQUES! I'D LIKE TO TALK A LITTLE ABOUT CHARACTER DESIGN AND DEVELOPMENT, FROM IDEA CONCEPT TO SKETCH TO FINAL VERSION! LET'S PROCEED...

THE "DRAGON PHARAOH" IS AN EXTREMELY POWERFUL CHARACTER I INTRODUCED DURING THE "NHS/GD CROSSOVER "TIMEWARP." I WANTED TO CREATE A BLACK CHARACTER WITH MYSTIC POWERS, SOMETHING WHICH YOU DON'T SEE VERY OFTEN. SO I MADE HIM AN EYGPTIAN PHARAOH AND DID A GREAT DEAL OF RESEARCH IN ORDER TO DESIGN HIM VERY AUTHENTICALLY IN REGARDS TO HIS LOOK AND COSTUME...

THESE ARE SOME OF THE FIRST DRAWINGS I DID. I THEN OPTED TO SAVE THESE DESIGNS FOR A LATER, MODERN-DAY VERSION OF THE DRAGON PHARAOH, WHICH I WILL ONE DAY INTRODUCE IF I CAN GIVE HIM A REASON FOR COMING BACK!

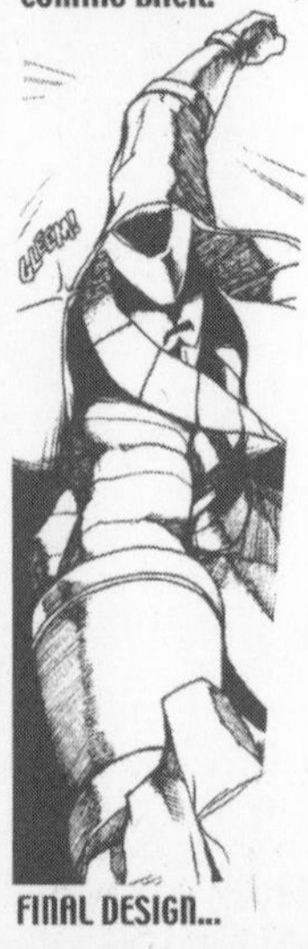

FINAL DESIGN...

CHARACTER DESIGN

THESE ARE CHARACTERS FROM "THE DYNASTY." I ENVISIONED THEM AS AN ANCIENT RACE WHO WERE MERGED WITH MACHINES AND HIGH TECHNOLOGY. I CHOSE NOT TO GO THE CYBORG ROUTE, LIKE MAKING THEM LOOK LIKE THE "BORG" FROM "STAR TREK." I ACTUALLY FOUND MY INSPIRATION IN THE WAY THE CHARACTERS WERE DESIGNED IN THE MOVIE "TRON." I LIKED THE IDEA OF INTEGRATING LIVING CIRCUITRY INTO A CHARACTER INSTEAD OF MAKING THEM LOOK LIKE YOUR TYPICAL MECHANICAL ROBOT/HUMAN MISH-MASH...

CHARACTER DESIGN

...AGAIN, MORE "DYNASTY" CHARACTERS. I TRIED TO GIVE THEM A VERY SIMILAR LOOK AND FEEL WHILE STILL TRYING TO MAKE THEM STAND ALONE SEPERATELY AS WELL. I ONLY WISH I HAD NAMED THEM A LITTLE MORE DIFFERENTLY; SINCE ALL OF THEIR NAMES SOUND THE SAME, MY READERS GOT THEM CONFUSED WITH EACH OTHER!

CHARACTER DESIGN

IN "GOLD DIGGER" I SET OUT TO CREATE A RACE OF MATTER-ABSORBING ENTITIES FROM ANOTHER DIMENSION THAT WOULD BE VERY CREEPY AND VERY MEMORABLE...
SO AS I BRAINSTORMED IDEAS, I CAME TO THE CONCLUSION THAT REALLY LONG, THIN-LIMBED CREATURES WOULD REALLY BE THE WAY TO GO.
I STRIVED FOR A SURREAL, SCARY APPROACH... THE SIMPLER I MADE THE FEATURES, THE MORE FRIGHTENING THE BETANS BECAME.
WOULD YOU WANT TO STUMBLE ACROSS ONE OF THESE THINGS IN A DARK ALLEY... I THINK NOT!

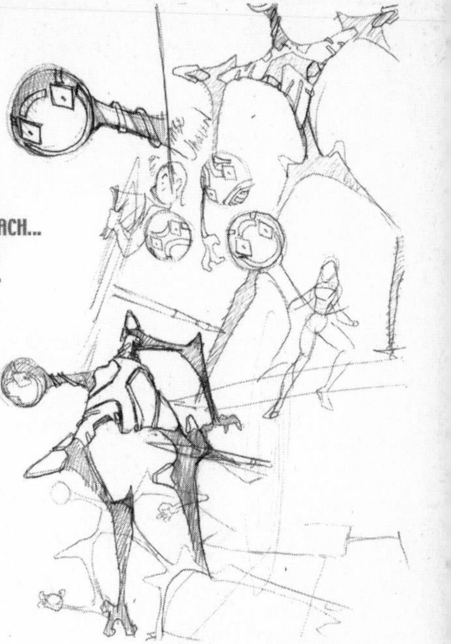

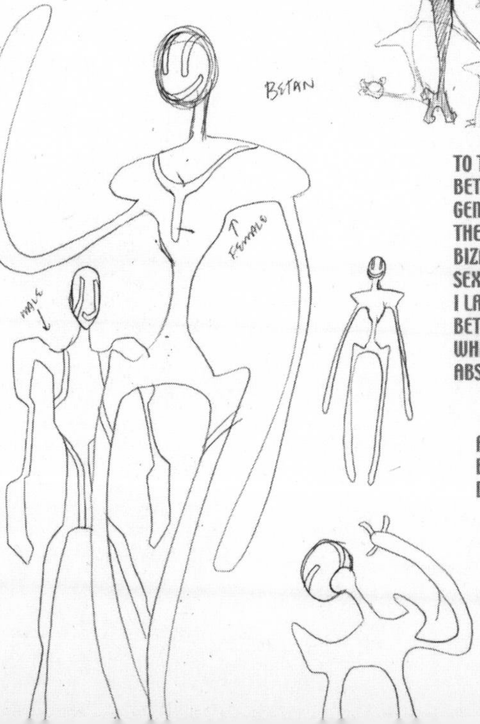

TO THE LEFT HERE, I DREW SOME BETAN STUDIES REGARDING GENDERS... THEN I THOUGHT, THESE THINGS ARE TOO BIZARRE TO HAVE ANY SEXUAL ORIENTATION...
I LATER REVISED THE "GENDER" BETA IDEA IN ORDER TO SHOW WHAT SEX THE PERSON ABSORBED BY THE BETAN WAS...

FINAL BETAN DESIGN

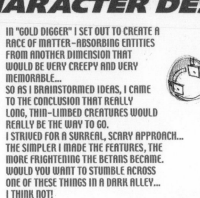

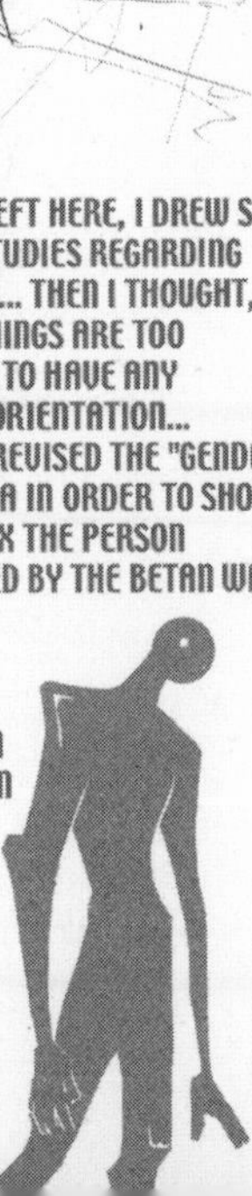

HOW TO DRAW MANGA: THE FRED PERRY WAY

CHARACTER DESIGN

ACTUAL BENJI

DR. PEACHBODY

MEAN BENJI! WHILE DOING "TIMEWARP" I HAD THE DIABOLICAL DR.PEACHBODY TAKE OVER BENJI'S FEEBLE MIND. BENJI IS DR.PEACHBODY'S "PET BOY," AN INNOCENT MIND THAT JUST DOES WHAT HIS MASTER SAYS.

INSTEAD OF THE HULKING, MANIACAL BENJI, I WENT WITH A "COMBO" OF THE TWO CHARACTERS TO FORM THE FINAL CREATION...I DO LIKE THE HULK BENJI THOUGH; HE'S ONE EVIL LOOKING DUDE!

FINAL BENJI/ PEACHBODY MONSTER

PRACTICE PAGE

HOW TO DRAW MANGA: THE FRED PERRY WAY
ADVANCED CONCEPTS: SPECIAL FX

FIRST OFF, LET'S START WITH A FIGHTING GAME-STYLE IMPACT FX...

BEFORE YOU DRAW THE SPECIAL EFFECTS, HOWEVER, YOU HAVE TO RENDER THE ACTION AND (MOST IMPORTANTLY) THE REACTION OF THE CHARACTERS.

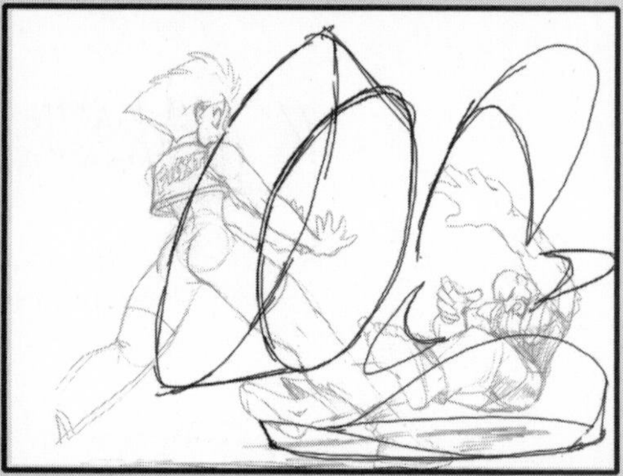

ONCE THAT'S DONE, IT'S TIME TO SKETCH OUT THE GUIDELINES FOR THE IMPACT FX...

HERE YOU CAN SEE I USE GEOMETRIC SHAPES TO OUTLINE THE IMPACT FX AREAS.

I TEND TO USE CONIC SHAPES AND CURVES FOR MY IMPACTS. AFTER TRYING OTHER SHAPES, I'VE HAD THE BEST RESULTS WITH THESE...

WITH THE GUIDELINES PLACED, IT'S EASY TO USE THE "FLASH-BURST" ON THE SHAPE AREAS TO CREATE THE IMPACT FX...

HOW TO DRAW MANGA: THE FRED PERRY WAY
ADVANCED CONCEPTS: SPECIAL FX

HERE IS AN EXAMPLE OF MY "FLASH BURST" TECHNIQUE. NOTE THAT THE FOCUS POINT BEGINS ON THE ARM BLOCK.

IN THIS EXAMPLE, THE "FLASH BURST" IS RENDERED VERY LARGE, PRACTICALLY ENGULFING THE CHARACTERS, THEREFORE INCREASING THE IMPACT AND DRAMA OF THE SCENE.

HOW TO DRAW MANGA: THE FRED PERRY WAY

ADVANCED CONCEPTS: SPECIAL FX

HERE'S AN EXAMPLE OF THE FLASH BURST AS USED TO CONVEY PSYCHIC POWERS.

PPEARS ERWIN AND
HAVE DEDUCED
UR CLAIRVOYANCE
VEALED TO US...
TUM
ELY
...
D AND
N THE
S OF
ION
DINARY

IN THIS SCENE, I USED IT TO SHOW HOW HER THRUSTERS ARE "KICKIN' UP DUST."

OH
YEA

AND OF COURSE, THE FLASH BURST TECHNIQUE IS IDEAL FOR PORTRAYING FIREBALLS. NOTICE THE WAY YOU CAN SEE THE CONCAVITY OR THE "BACK" OF THE FIREBALL, WHICH IS ACTUALLY MORE OF A DOME SHAPE AS SEEN HERE.

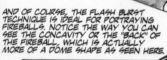

GASP!!
SHF-SHUHS

HOW TO DRAW MANGA: THE FRED PERRY WAY

ADVANCED CONCEPTS: SPECIAL FX

TO THE RIGHT, WE HAVE AN EXAMPLE OF THE IMPACT OF SOMEONE HITTING THE GROUND. IT'S ALWAYS GOOD TO CONVEY THE CONSEQUENCE TO A CERTAIN ACTION.

IN THE PANEL BELOW, I UTILIZE THE TECHNIQUE TO ILLUSTRATE "CHI" ENERGY GROWING BETWEEN CHARACTER'S HANDS.

ABOVE, I USED IT TO ILLUSTRATE THE PATH THE CAR IS TAKING. I THINK YOU CAN GET A REAL SENSE THAT IT'S IN A HURRY AND MOVIN' OUT.

PRACTICE PAGE

HOW TO DRAW MANGA: THE FRED PERRY WAY
ADVANCED CONCEPTS: SPECIAL FX

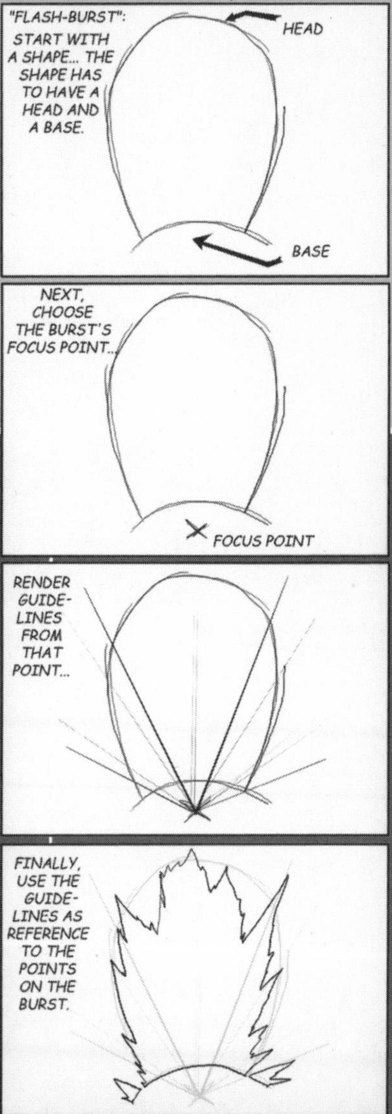

"FLASH-BURST":
START WITH A SHAPE... THE SHAPE HAS TO HAVE A HEAD AND A BASE.
HEAD
BASE
NEXT, CHOOSE THE BURST'S FOCUS POINT...
FOCUS POINT
RENDER GUIDE-LINES FROM THAT POINT...
FINALLY, USE THE GUIDE-LINES AS REFERENCE TO THE POINTS ON THE BURST.

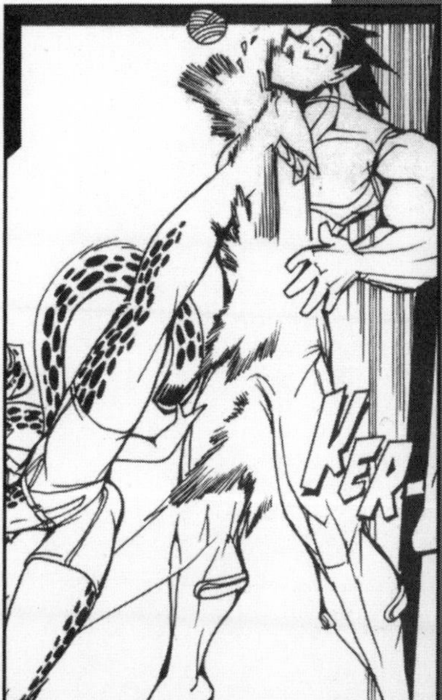

KER-

I LIKE THE WAY THESE FLASHBURSTS REALLY GET ACROSS THE VIOLENCE OF THE GUNFIRE. THEY'RE REALLY DRASTIC AND POWERFUL HERE.

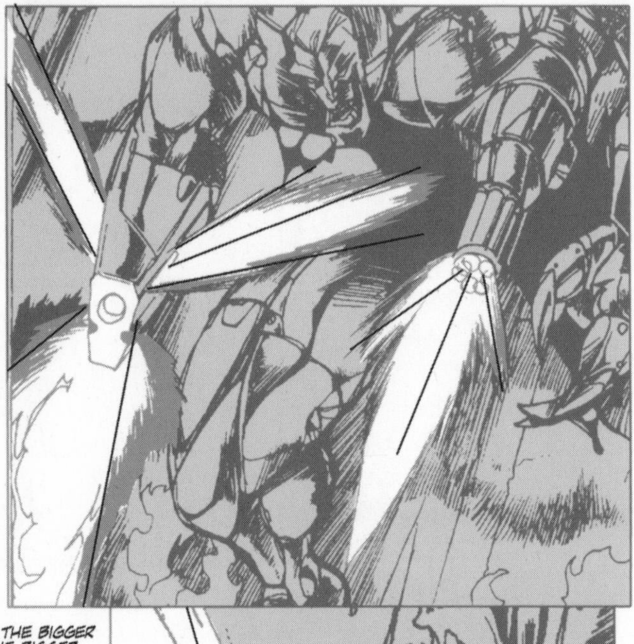

REMEMBER, THE BIGGER THE GUN, THE BIGGER THE MUZZLE FLASH.

NOTE THE DIRECTIONAL LINES THAT ARE USED AS GUIDELINES FOR THE MUZZLE FLASH.

IN THE SHOT UNDERNEATH, YOU CAN SEE A COMBINATION OF MUZZLE FLASH AND AN IMPACT EFFECT AROUND IT TO ILLUSTRATE THE WEAPON'S POWERFUL SHOCKWAVE STYLE BURST.

AS YOU CAN SEE, MUZZLE FLASHES CAN BE DONE IN A WIDE VARIETY OF WAYS.

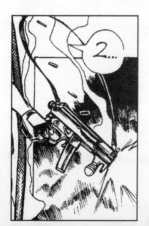

ADVANCED CONCEPTS: SPECIAL FX

TO THE LEFT, WE HAVE WHAT BASICALLY AMOUNTS TO DIRECTED ENERGY EFFECTS, MOSTLY USED TO CLEARLY DEMONSTRATE THE DIRECTION OR PATH OF AN ENERGY BOLT OR DISCHARGE.

BELOW: ANOTHER EXAMPLE OF A DIRECTIONAL EFFECT.

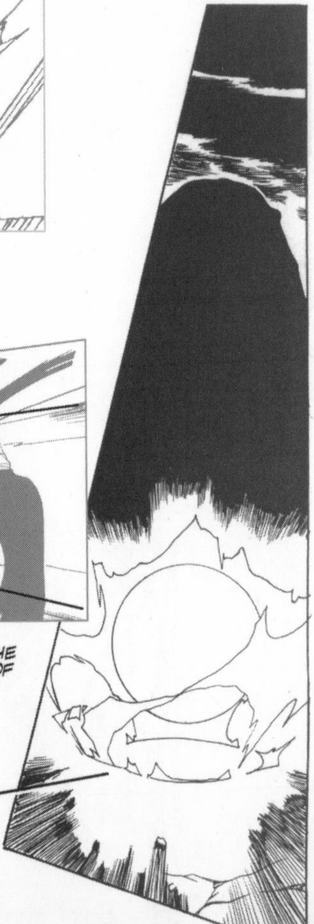

ON THE RIGHT WE HAVE A SPHERICAL VERSION OF THE FLASH BURST TECHNIQUE. NOTE HOW THE BOTTOM OF THE EFFECT INDICATES THE CENTRAL OBJECT'S RELATIONSHIP AND DISTANCE TO THE GROUND.

DETAILED CLOSE-UP.

PRACTICE PAGE

HOW TO DRAW MANGA: THE FRED PERRY WAY

ADVANCED CONCEPTS: SPECIAL FX

"AIRY-CROSSHATCH": THIS IS THE BASE FOR SMOKE'S TEXTURE.

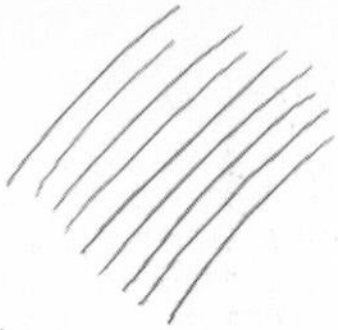

START WITH PARALLEL LINES...

NOW, AT A SLIGHTLY OFF ANGLE, CROSS THOSE LINES SO THAT THE TIPS FORM LITTLE PARALLEL-OGRAMS.

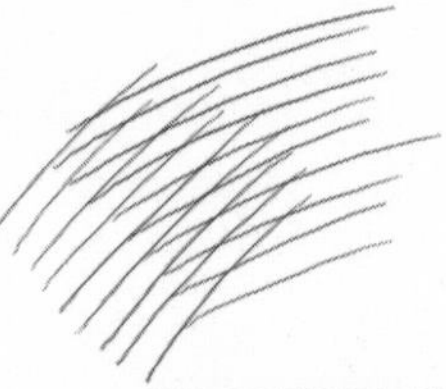

THIS PATTERN MAKES IT DARKER IN THE MIDDLE AND LIGHT ON BOTH ENDS.

"SMOKE":

RENDER A PUFFY SHAPE FOR THE CLOUD...

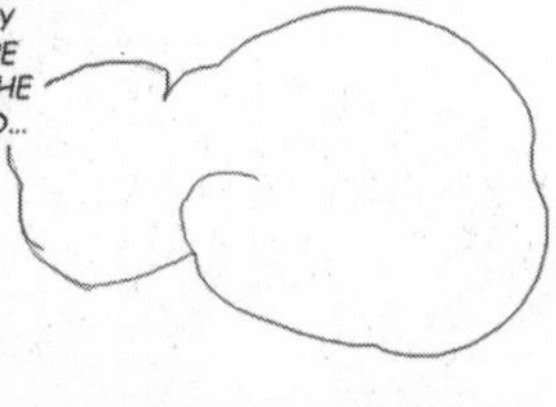

NOW, ADD TEXTURE USING THE "AIRY-CROSSHATCH"...

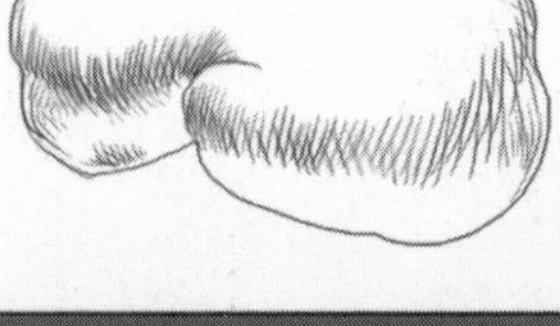

ON THE RIGHT, WE HAVE SOMETHING LIKE A VORTEX EFFECT TAKING PLACE IN THE SKY. BASICALLY, I'M APPLYING THE TECHNIQUE FOR THE FLASH BURST WITH MY CLOUDS.

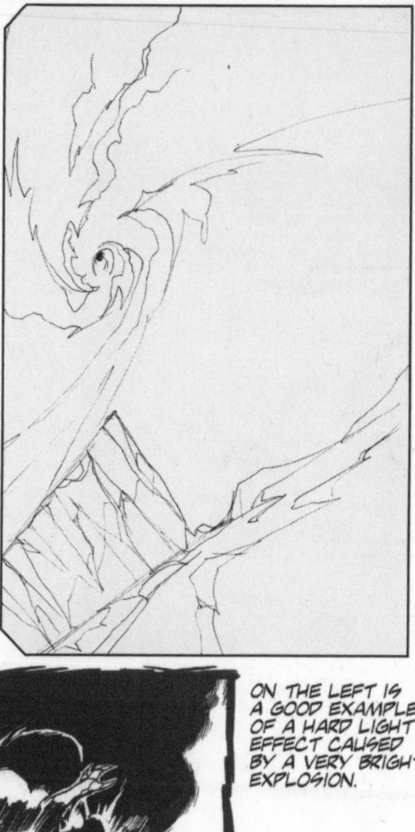

ON THE LEFT IS A GOOD EXAMPLE OF A HARD LIGHT EFFECT CAUSED BY A VERY BRIGHT EXPLOSION.

ON THIS PAGE ARE SOME PRACTICE FLASH BURSTS. I'M USUALLY ALWAYS TRYING TO PERFECT THEM OR LEARN SOMETHING NEW TO BETTER ILLUSTRATE THE EFFECT I'M TRYING TO COMMUNICATE.

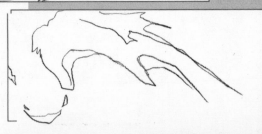

NOW WE'LL HAVE AN EXAMPLE OF THE "FLASH-BURST" AND "SMOKE" FX.

FIRST RENDER THE DRAWING THAT MAY HAVE BOTH FX...

I DECIDED ON HAVING A SOLDIER SHOOTING IT OUT IN SMOKING SURROUNDINGS.

RENDER THE GUIDE-LINES FOR THE SMOKE AND THE FLASH-BURST OF HIS WEAPON...

NEXT, USING THE GUIDELINE AROUND THE MUZZLE, RENDER A SIMPLE "FLASH-BURST".

NOW CREATE SOME FOREGROUND CLOUDS WITHIN THE CLOUD GUIDELINE...

THESE CLOUDS WILL BE SHADED LIGHTER THAN THE AREAS OF THE MAIN CLOUD TO GIVE IT A 3D FEEL.

FINALLY, USE THE FEATHER CROSSHATCH TO FLESH OUT THE DETAILS IN THE CLOUDS.

TRY NOT TO OVERPOWER THE SOLDIER WITH THE CLOUD'S DETAILS... THE MAIN CHARACTER MAY GET LOST IN THE PICTURE IF YOU GO OVERBOARD.

SOMETIMES ADDING LINE WEIGHT CAN HELP DISTINGUISH A CHARACTER FROM A BUSY BACKGROUND...

PRACTICE PAGE

LET'S TALK ABOUT DRAWING A PAGE FROM START TO FINISH AND SOME OF THE VARIOUS TECHNIQUES I USE IN THE PROCESS.

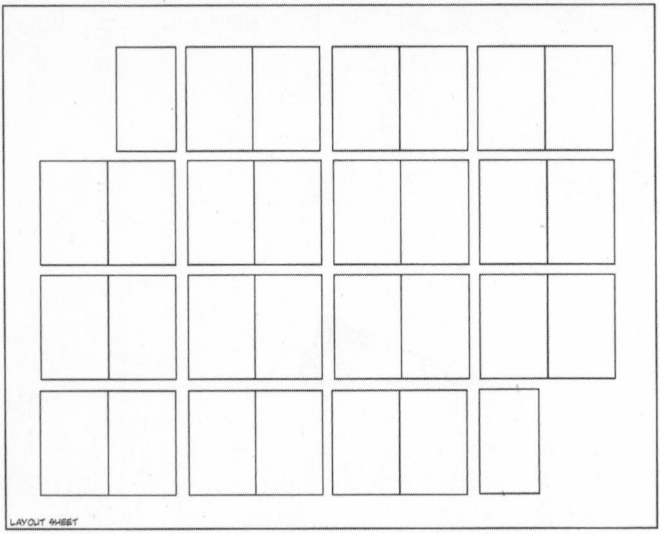

NOW, I'VE GOT MY LAYOUT SHEET AND I'LL START DRAWING THUMBNAILS OF THE STORY. FOR THE MOST PART, I'LL EITHER DRAW A FULL SKETCH AT THIS POINT OR I'LL ENLARGE THE IMAGE ON THE COPIER.

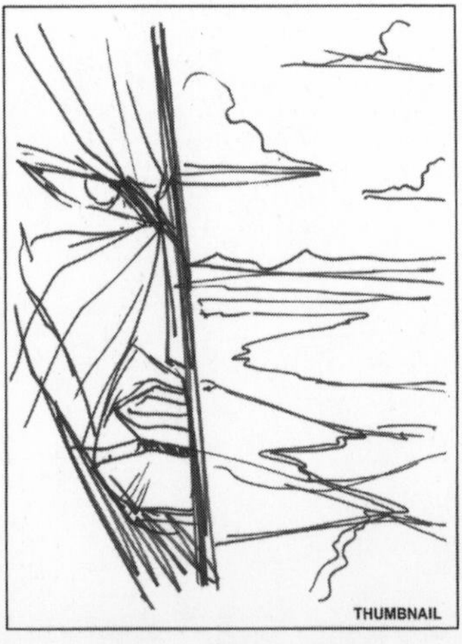

NOW TO HIT THE LIGHT TABLE. IT'S NOT REALLY THAT DIFFICULT TO USE THE LIGHT TABLE TO REFINE YOUR ILLUSTRATIONS, AND I GENERALLY PREFER IT.

OFTEN I WILL DO A THUMBNAIL VERSION OF A PAGE, AND I END UP LIKING THE THUMBNAIL VERSION BETTER THAN THE FINAL PENCILS. SOMETIMES THE IMMEDIACY AND FLOW OF THE IMAGE WORKS BETTER IN THAT ORIGINAL SKETCH, SO I JUST ENLARGE THE PIECE AND SAVE MYSELF SOME TIME AND TROUBLE.

THUMBNAIL

I BEGAN THE PAGE WITH THE THUMBNAIL AT THE LEFT. I REALLY LIKED THE LAYOUT, SO I STARTED PENCILING THE PAGE RIGHT AWAY. AS THE PENCILS PROGRESSED, I FOUND THAT I WASN'T GETTING WHAT I WANTED. I REDREW THE IMAGE A COUPLE OF TIMES, AND THE PAGE JUST WASN'T CLICKING. LATER, I DECIDED TO USE THE THUMBNAIL SKETCH THAT I'D STARTED OUT WITH, AND THE PAGE ENDED UP WORKING OUT AS WELL AS I HAD HOPED.

PENCILS-FIRST ATTEMPT

FINAL PAGE

TIGHT SKETCH

AS FAR AS THUMBNAILS GO, FOR ME THEY RANGE FROM HIGHLY DETAILED TO VERY, VERY LOOSE. IT REALLY DEPENDS ON MY STATE OF MIND AT THE TIME. IT ALSO DEPENDS OF THE TYPE OF PEN I'M USING. SOMETIMES I'LL USE A SHARPIE MARKER AND OTHERS I'LL USE A FINE PEN. THERE ARE NO HARD AND FAST RULES HERE.

IN THE FOLLOWING EXAMPLE, I'LL SHOW YOU HOW I TAKE A PAGE FROM THUMB-NAIL TO FINISHED TONED IMAGE!

THUMBNAIL TRACE:

IN ORDER TO ENLARGE MY THUMBNAIL TO THE PROPER SIZE, I SCANNED THE IMAGE INTO MY COMPUTER. THE REASON I USED THE COMPUTER INSTEAD OF A PHOTOCOPIER IS THAT I CAN MORE QUICKLY AND EASILY DO IT ON THE COMPUTER. WITH A COPIER IT MAY TAKE ME SEVERAL TRIES AND MULTIPLE SHEETS OF PAPER TO GET THE SIZE I WANT. IN THE COMPUTER, I CAN INPUT THE EXACT SIZE I NEED AND PRINT IT OUT ON ONE OR TWO SHEETS!

THEN JUST DROP IT ON THE LIGHT TABLE AND START PENCILLING! WITH A GUIDE AS LOOSE AS WHAT I STARTED OUT WITH, I TOOK SOME TIME TO REFINE THE IMAGE AND ADD SOME FEATURES TO THE PAGE AS WELL.

ON THE VILLAIN'S FACE, I REFINED AND SHARPENED UP HIS FEATURES AND REDUCED HIS JAWLINE. I THOUGHT THE CHIN WAS A BIT TOO LONG. FOR THE LANDSCAPE I WENT AHEAD AND ADDED A WATERFALL BECAUSE IT LEADS INTO THE NEXT SCENE. YOU SHOULD TRY TO BE AWARE OF OPPORTUNITES TO AID THE FLOW OF THE STORY AND PLACES TO MAKE THE STORY EASIER TO FOLLOW.

HOW TO DRAW MANGA

NOW, ON TO THE INKING. SOME OUT THERE MIGHT WANT TO KNOW WHAT I USE TO INK. SIMPLY PUT, YOU CAN USE ANYTHING THAT PUTS INK ON A PAGE--BALLPOINT PEN, BRUSH, MARKERS, WHATEVER...

PERSONALLY, I USE ZIG FINE LINE MARKERS, .005. THEY HARDLY BLEED OR SMEAR, AND ARE ALSO FAIRLY INEXPENSIVE. OF COURSE, I DON'T KNOW WHERE MY RENT IS COMING FROM THIS MONTH. OH WELL...

THINGS GO PRETTY FAST FROM HERE. AFTER SCANNING IN THE PIECE, I START TONING IT.

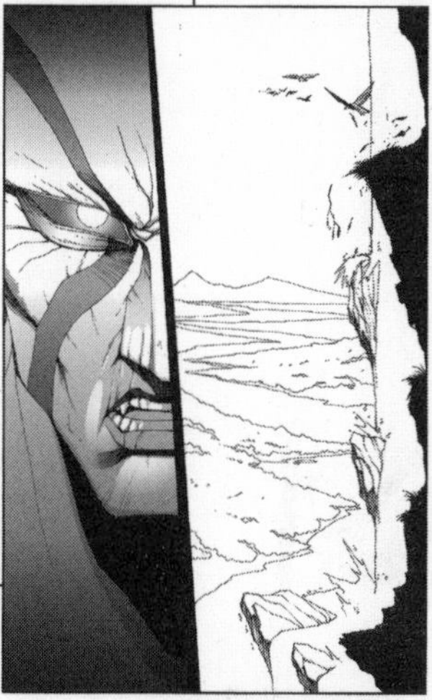

THE TONING IS FAIRLY EASY. JUST GO WITH YOUR OWN TASTES.

IN MY CASE, I TONE USING THE SAME TECHNIQUE AS IN COLORING. I LAY DOWN TONE IN DIFFERENT AREAS IN VARIOUS SHADES IN ORDER TO BETTER SEPARATE THE PICTURE FOR FURTHER SHADING.

I DIDN'T START RECORDING MY PROGRESS UNTIL HALFWAY THROUGH THE PAGE...

IN THE PROCESS OF LAYING DOWN AREAS OF GRAY TONE.

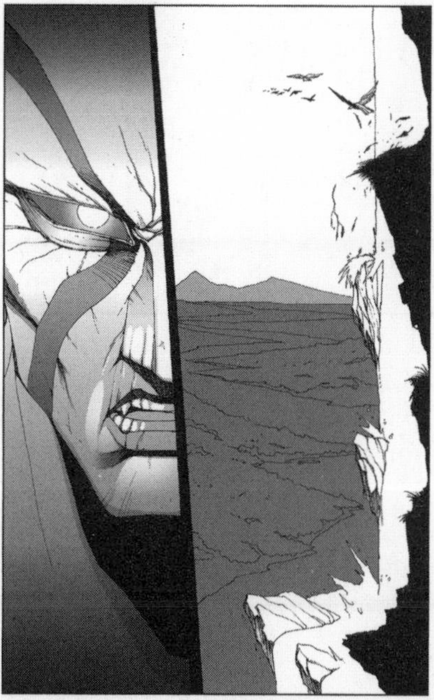

ADDING HIGHLIGHTS TO THE RIVER-

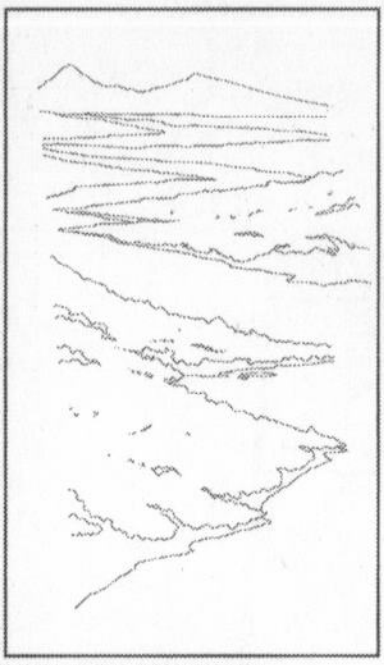

LINEWORK SELECTION-

NOW THAT I'VE LAYED OUT THE AREAS OF TONE, I START SELECTING WITH THE LASSO TOOL TO HIGHLIGHT AND SHADE, DEPENDING ON WHAT I NEED.

I ALSO START SELECTING LINEWORK AND LIGHTEN ITS TONE IN ORDER TO ADD TO THE SENSE OF DISTANCE IN THE PANEL.

STARTING HIGHLIGHTS ON THE CLOUDBANK-

FINAL CLOUDBANK-

THE WATERFALL WAS THE MOST DIFFICULT PART OF THE PANEL TO TONE. I HAD TO SPEND A LONG TIME CHANGING THE BRIGHTNESS AND CONTRAST TO GET IT THE WAY I WANTED IT.

FINAL PANEL-

AT THIS POINT, I'M ALMOST DONE. I BLUR THE DISTANT OBJECTS IN THE BACK-GROUND AND THEN I TINKER WITH THE TONES IN THE BACKGROUND TO MAKE IT SEEM EVEN FURTHER AWAY.

AND HERE WE HAVE THE FINAL PRODUCT! I'M SURE I HAVE LEFT YOU WITH MORE QUESTIONS THAN ANSWERS, BUT IT'S A BEGINNING. LATER, I WILL GIVE OUT SOME TIPS ON HOW TO CREATE YOUR OWN SCREENTONES ON THE 'PUTER!

PRACTICE PAGE

HOW TO DRAW MANGA

CUTE ENGINE
DESIGNING CUTE GIRLS FOR MANGA
A COUPLE OF QUICK NOTES: START A SKETCHBOOK IF YOU HAVEN'T ALREADY. IT'S A GREAT PLACE TO GET YOUR IDEAS OUT ON PAPER. TRY TO WORK IN YOUR SKETCHBOOK EVERY DAY. YOU'LL THANK ME LATER.
REFERENCE, REFERENCE, REFERENCE, IT CAN'T BE SAID ENOUGH. IT'S A NECESSARY TOOL, AND YOU ARE GOING TO NEED IT IF YOU WANT TO EMULATE JAPANESE MANGA. DON'T JUST GLANCE AT YOUR COPY OF "DARK MINDS" OR SOME JOE MAD STUFF YOU'VE GOT LAYING AROUND.
YOU NEED THE STUFF ADAM WARREN, PAT LEE, OR FRED PERRY GET THEIR INSPIRATION FROM!
NOW, IF YOU'RE LUCKY, YOU HAVE A LOCAL COMIC SHOP THAT CARRIES SOME MANGA. BUT KEEP AN EYE OPEN, YOU NEVER KNOW WHEN SOMETHING WILL CATCH YOUR EYE!

OKAY, LET'S GET STARTED. WE'LL COME UP WITH THE BODY FIRST. WHATEVER YOU FEEL IS RIGHT FOR YOUR CHARACTER. IN THIS CASE, I WANTED A SEMI-ATHLETIC FIGURE. I PUT HER IN THE POSE SHE'S IN BECAUSE THERE IS NOTHING AS BORING AS THE STANDARD STATIC MANIQUIN POSE I OFTEN SEE FOLKS USE WHEN THEY FIRST DESIGN A CHARACTER. I UNDERSTAND THE PRACTICAL REASONS FOR THOSE POSES, BUT I WANTED SOMETHING A LITTLE FLASHY HERE.

ANOTHER REASON TO HAVE THE CHARACTER IN A POSE LIKE THIS IS THAT IT CAN HELP IN THE DESIGN PROCESS. THIS POSE MADE ME WANT TO PUT TAILS ON HER RIGHT AWAY TO HELP WITH THE FLOW OF THE IMAGE. BY THAT TIME I PRETTY MUCH KNEW WHAT I WANTED TO DO WITH THE CHARACTER.

INSTEAD OF RUNNING, IT LOOKED MORE LIKE SHE'S POISED TO STRIKE. SO I DECIDE TO DO A CHUN LI INSPIRED CHARACTER. I DID THE FACE FIRST TO GIVE A PROPER LOOK. THEN, I DID THE SHOULDERS. I SEEM TO LIKE THE PUFFY SHOULDERS FOR SOME REASON... WHEN I DID THE SLEEVES, I HAD THE DESIGN ELEMENT I NEEDED TO FINISH THE DESIGN

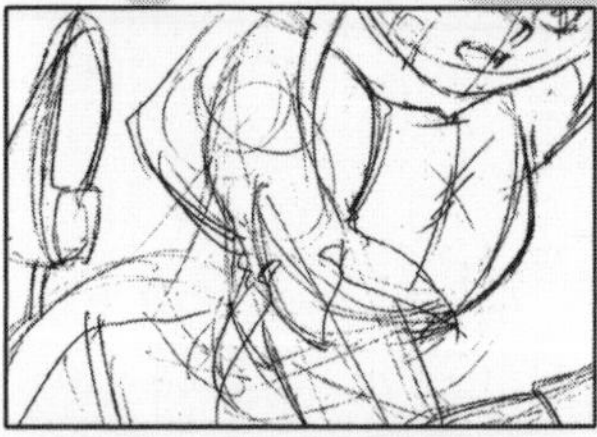

I SEEMED TO REMEMBER THAT CHUN LI HAD SLEEVES SIMILAR TO THESE, AND THEY WERE SO RIGHT I TRIED TO REUSE THE SAME SHAPE THROUGHOUT THE COSTUME.

YOU MIGHT HAVE NOTICED THE LITTLE CIRCLE I DREW IN THE CENTER OF OUR FIGHTER'S FOREHEAD... I DRAW THAT AS SORT OF AN ANCHOR FOR THE HAIR. IN THIS CASE, THE GIRL'S BANGS.

WELL, HERE ARE THE FINISHED PENCILS FOR THIS DESIGN. IT LOOKS PRETTY GOOD. I DECIDED NOT INK IT BECAUSE I'M AFRAID I MIGHT MESS IT UP!
HMMM... Y'KNOW, I WAS GOING TO GIVE HER A SCAR, BUT I THINK THE BAND-AIDS ARE A NICE TOUCH.
BY THE WAY, I USED A LIGHTBOX ON THIS PICTURE TO GET REALLY CLEAN AND TIGHT PENCILS.

LET'S TRY ANOTHER FIGHTER-TYPE, SHALL WE? THIS DESIGN IS DIFFERENT FROM MOST OF MY OTHER WORK. THIS ONE SHOWS A LOT MORE JAPANESE INFLUENCE. MAYBE THIS IS WHERE MY STYLE IS HEADED IN THE FUTURE. SHE LOOKS LIKE SHE'S READY TO WORK IN A VIDEO GAME OR MAYBE AN ANIME?

IN THIS CASE, I ANCHORED THE HAIR TO AN ARBITRARY POINT AWAY FROM THE HEAD, INSTEAD OF ON THE FOREHEAD AS I NORMALLY DO. I KIND OF SCULPTED THE GENERAL SHAPE OF THE HAIR BEFORE REALLY DRAWING IT. THIS IS ONE OF THE FEW CHARACTERS I'VE DRAWN THAT WEARS GLASSES. I THOUGHT SOME LITTLE SPECTACLES HANGING OFF THE NOSE MIGHT BUMP UP THE CUTE-FACTOR.

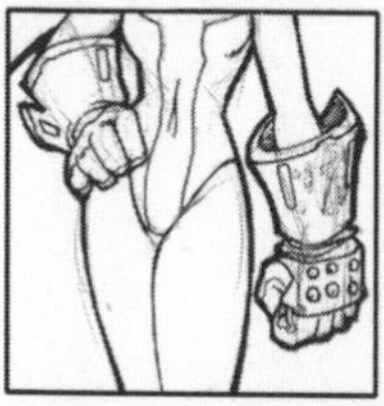

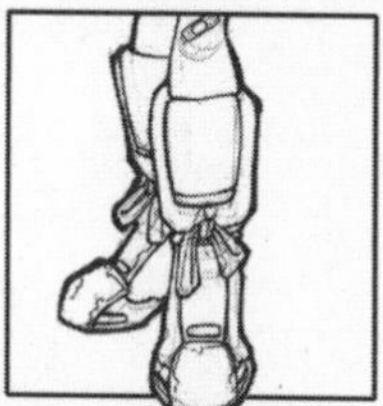

RIGHT NOW I'M A BIG FAN OF OVER-SIZED PROPS. NOT JUST MALLETS, THOUGH, YOU CAN MAKE ANYTHING OVER-SIZED TO ADD TO YOUR CHARACTER. THE BIG GLOVES ENHANCE THE WHOLE "VIDEO GAME" LOOK. YOU MIGHT BE ABLE TO NOTICE THE MARKS ON THE BACK OF ONE GLOVE. I WAS ORIGINALLY GOING TO GIVE THEM SOME KIND OF MAGICAL POWERS. OOOO... A LITTLE TOO MUCH "BATTLE CHASERS" IN MY DIET. AS FOR THE BOOTS, I'VE BEEN HAVING SOME SUCCESS AT USING OVER-SIZED BOOTS ON SOME OF MY CHARACTERS, AND I THINK THEY WERE USED TO GOOD EFFECT HERE!

THINGS TO NOTE:

THIS SKETCH WAS REALIZED FAIRLY QUICKLY. MOST OF THE ELEMENTS I USED ARE BASED OFF OF CONCEPTS I'VE SEEN USED TO GREAT EFFECT BY JAPANESE ARTISTS. THROUGH OBSERVATION, AND PRACTICE I THINK I'VE MANAGED TO GET A SMALL DEGREE OF WHAT I WAS LOOKING FOR WITH THIS PIECE. LIKE I SAID, THE HAIR IS PRETTY NEW FOR ME. IF YOU LOOK AT THE SKETCH, YOU CAN SEE I ORIGINALY HAD THE HAIR GOING DOWN HER BACK. I SUPPOSE I SHOULD MENTION SOMETHING ABOUT THE CHARACTER'S BUST. NO, YOUR CHARACTERS DO NOT HAVE TO HAVE LAURA CROFT'S FIGURE IN ORDER TO LOOK GOOD. THE TREND AT THE MOMENT IS TOWARD A LARGE BUST, THAT COULD CHANGE. I PERSONALLY DON'T LIKE TO DRAW GIRLS WITH A BIG CHEST (I DON'T DRAW LARGE BUSTS VERY WELL) BASICALY, THAT IS UP TO YOU. YOU HAVE TO DECIDE IF A CERTAIN BODY TYPE WILL ADD TO, OR DETRACT FROM YOUR CHARACTER DESIGN.

AND HERE IS THE FINAL ART, INKED AND READY FOR COLOURING! THIS IS A PICTURE I'M PRETTY HAPPY WITH. IT'S NEAT, CLEAN, AND SIMPLE. I ALSO LIKE IT BECAUSE I SHOWS MORE OF MY STRENGTHS THAN MY WEAKNESSES. AND, OF COURSE THE BAND-AID MAKES ANOTHER SHOWING. NOW LIKE I SAID, THIS IS A SIMPLE DESIGN. THERE IS NOTHING TO STOP YOU FROM GOING NUTS WITH YOUR DESIGNS. I TEND TO BE A LITTLE BIT MORE RESEVED THAN MOST, BUT I AM SLOWLY COMING OUT OF THAT. IN FACT, I ADVOCATE GOING A LITTLE OVERBOARD WITH YOUR DESIGNS.

AGAIN, I USED THE LIGHTBOX TO POLISH OFF THE DESIGN. I NORMALLY ONLY USE THE LIGHTBOX WHEN I HAVE A SKETCH THAT I DON'T HAVE THE TIME TO REDRAW.

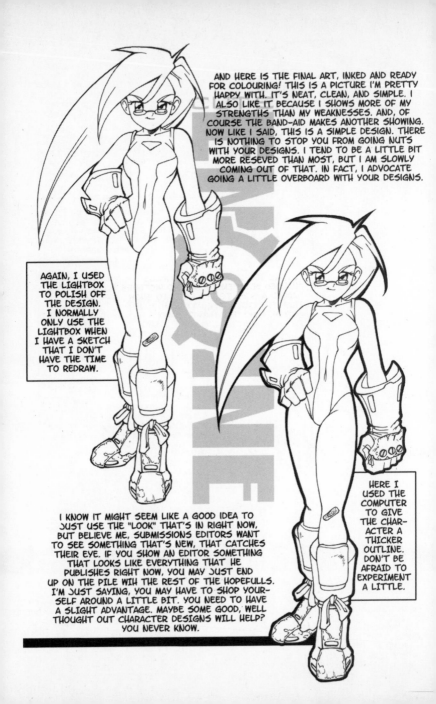

HERE I USED THE COMPUTER TO GIVE THE CHAR-ACTER A THICKER OUTLINE. DON'T BE AFRAID TO EXPERIMENT A LITTLE.

I KNOW IT MIGHT SEEM LIKE A GOOD IDEA TO JUST USE THE "LOOK" THAT'S IN RIGHT NOW, BUT BELIEVE ME, SUBMISSIONS EDITORS WANT TO SEE SOMETHING THAT'S NEW, THAT CATCHES THEIR EYE. IF YOU SHOW AN EDITOR SOMETHING THAT LOOKS LIKE EVERYTHING THAT HE PUBLISHES RIGHT NOW, YOU MAY JUST END UP ON THE PILE WIH THE REST OF THE HOPEFULLS. I'M JUST SAYING, YOU MAY HAVE TO SHOP YOUR-SELF AROUND A LITTLE BIT. YOU NEED TO HAVE A SLIGHT ADVANTAGE. MAYBE SOME GOOD, WELL THOUGHT OUT CHARACTER DESIGNS WILL HELP? YOU NEVER KNOW.

OKAY, NOW THAT THE JUICES ARE FLOWING A BIT, LET'S TRY A CHARACTER THAT'S A LITTLE MORE GROUNDED IN REALITY. MAYBE AN GUERRILLA FIGHTER FROM SOMETIME IN THE NEAR FUTURE! NOW MAYBE THE CHARACTER ISN'T AS TRUE TO LIFE AS MOST BUT WE ARE GOING FOR CUTE, REMEMBER? ONE OF THE THINGS YOU SHOULD KEEP AN EYE ON ARE THE CHARACTER'S PROPORTIONS. I GAVE HER A LARGE HEAD IN ORDER TO MAKE HER LOOK YOUNGER. I ALSO GAVE HER SOME FAIRLY LARGE BOOTS. IN THIS FIRST SKETCH, I GOT PRETTY MUCH WHAT I WANTED, AND I WAS HAPPY WITH IT. ALL OF THE ELEMENTS WORK WELL FOR THE PIECE. BUT, AS YOU CAN SEE SOME THINGS CHANGED BETWEEN THESE TWO PICTURES. I ADDED A SCAR TO HER FACE, TO SHOW THAT THE CHARACTER HAD SEEN SOME ACTION. ALSO, THE MIGHTY SABO THOUGHT THE GUN ON HER BACK LOOKED A LITTLE WEAK, SO I REFED A NEW ONE.

NOW, THE PIECE IS COMING ALONG. NOW I'LL LIGHTBOX THE DRAWING AND INK IT!

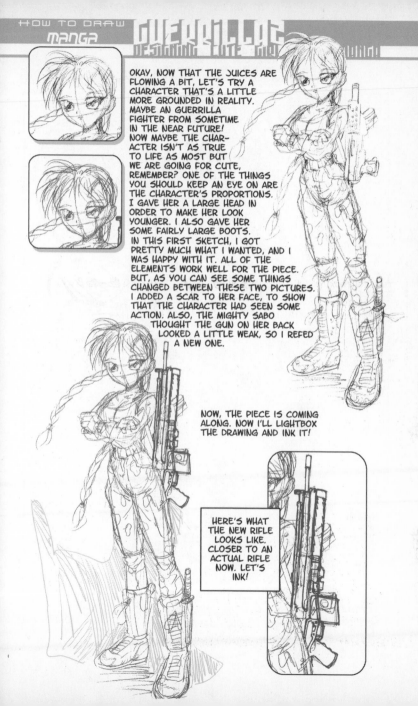

HERE'S WHAT THE NEW RIFLE LOOKS LIKE. CLOSER TO AN ACTUAL RIFLE NOW. LET'S INK!

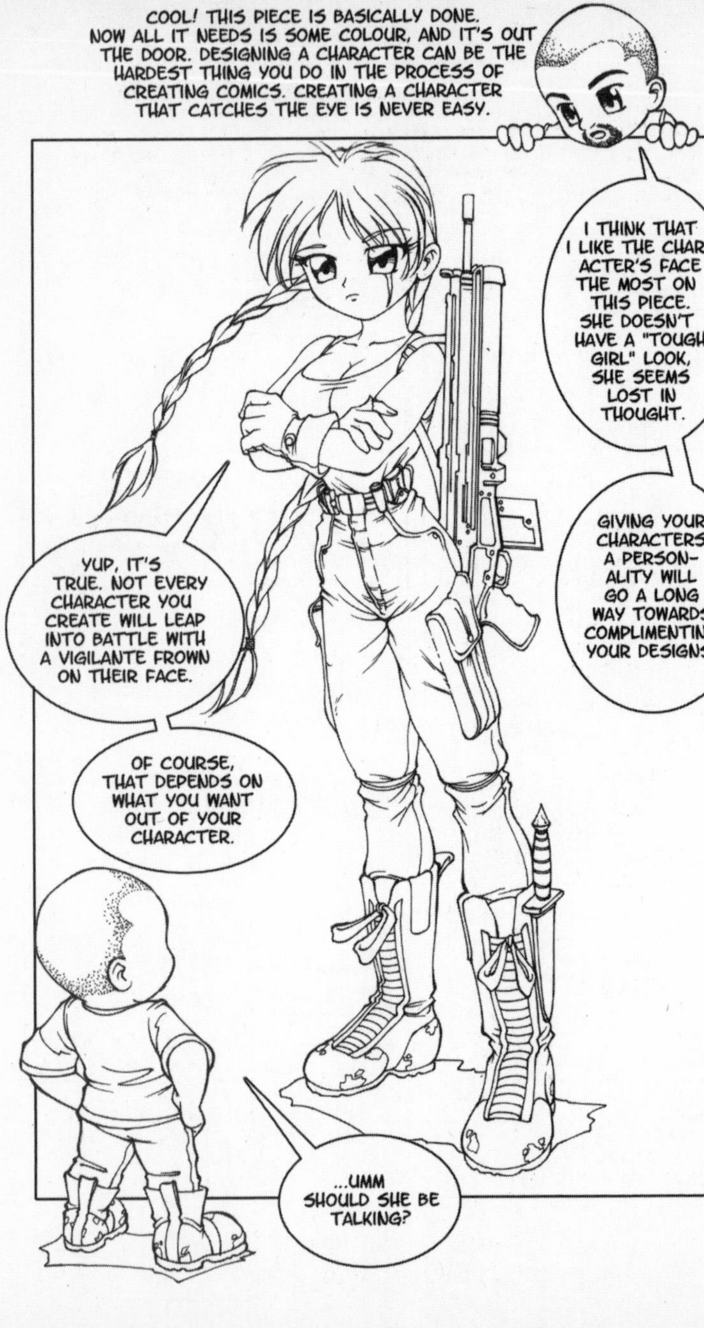
COOL! THIS PIECE IS BASICALLY DONE. NOW ALL IT NEEDS IS SOME COLOUR, AND IT'S OUT THE DOOR. DESIGNING A CHARACTER CAN BE THE HARDEST THING YOU DO IN THE PROCESS OF CREATING COMICS. CREATING A CHARACTER THAT CATCHES THE EYE IS NEVER EASY.
I THINK THAT I LIKE THE CHARACTER'S FACE THE MOST ON THIS PIECE. SHE DOESN'T HAVE A "TOUGH GIRL" LOOK, SHE SEEMS LOST IN THOUGHT.
GIVING YOUR CHARACTERS A PERSONALITY WILL GO A LONG WAY TOWARDS COMPLIMENTING YOUR DESIGNS.
YUP, IT'S TRUE. NOT EVERY CHARACTER YOU CREATE WILL LEAP INTO BATTLE WITH A VIGILANTE FROWN ON THEIR FACE.
OF COURSE, THAT DEPENDS ON WHAT YOU WANT OUT OF YOUR CHARACTER.
...UMM SHOULD SHE BE TALKING?

MOST ARTISTS DON'T LIKE TO ACKNOWLEDGE THEIR FORMATIVE WORK. ME? I'M DIFFERENT. I'M A FIRM BELIEVER IN REMEMBERING MY PAST WORKS. NOW, WHAT WE HAVE HERE ARE TWO DIFFERENT STYLES FROM TWO DIFFERENT PERIODS IN MY CAREER. WOW, A LOT OF THINGS ABOUT MY STYLE HAVE CHANGED, AND YET YOU CAN STILL SEE SOME OF THE COMMON THREADS THAT RUN THROUGH MY ART IN BOTH OF THESE PIECES.

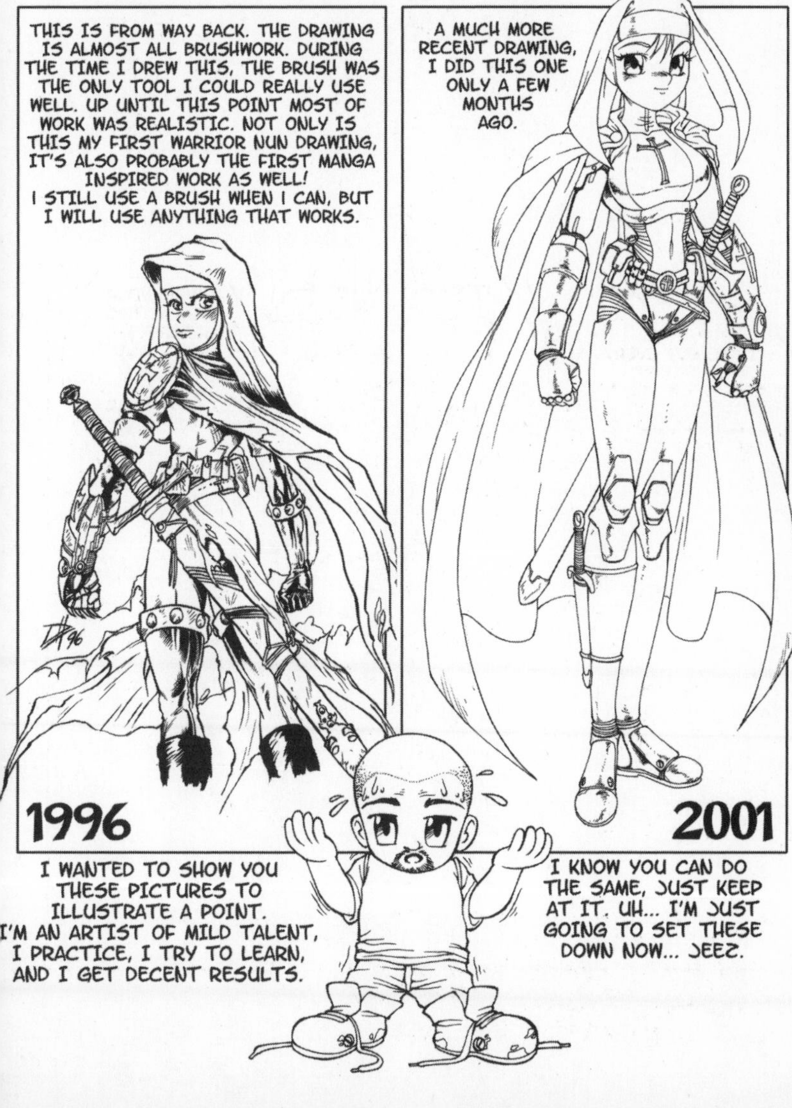

THIS IS FROM WAY BACK. THE DRAWING IS ALMOST ALL BRUSHWORK. DURING THE TIME I DREW THIS, THE BRUSH WAS THE ONLY TOOL I COULD REALLY USE WELL. UP UNTIL THIS POINT MOST OF WORK WAS REALISTIC. NOT ONLY IS THIS MY FIRST WARRIOR NUN DRAWING, IT'S ALSO PROBABLY THE FIRST MANGA INSPIRED WORK AS WELL!
I STILL USE A BRUSH WHEN I CAN, BUT I WILL USE ANYTHING THAT WORKS.
1996
A MUCH MORE RECENT DRAWING, I DID THIS ONE ONLY A FEW MONTHS AGO.
2001
I WANTED TO SHOW YOU THESE PICTURES TO ILLUSTRATE A POINT. I'M AN ARTIST OF MILD TALENT, I PRACTICE, I TRY TO LEARN, AND I GET DECENT RESULTS.
I KNOW YOU CAN DO THE SAME, JUST KEEP AT IT. UH... I'M JUST GOING TO SET THESE DOWN NOW... JEEZ.

PRACTICE PAGE

I DID THESE SKETCHES ON THE WAY BACK FROM A COMIC CONVENTION. THEY GO A LONG WAY TOWARD SETTING THE MOOD FOR THE CHARACTER AND HER WORLD. AT THIS POINT, THERE ARE SOME THINGS I WOULD LIKE TO CHANGE.

IN THE FIRST SKETCH, I THINK I'M ON THE RIGHT TRACK. MAYBE THE FACE COULD'VE BEEN BETTER, BUT I WAS RIDING IN A TRUCK AT THE TIME.

I HAVE SOME PROBLEMS WITH THE NEXT SKETCH. THE PROPORTIONS ARE WAY OFF. THE HAIR IS SO BAD THAT I ACTUALLY DECIDED TO DROP IT AND TRY A DIFFERENT STYLE! ALSO THE COSTUME REALLY NEEDS TO BE THOUGHT OUT A BIT MORE.
AT THIS POINT, I'M HAPPY WITH THE PROGRESS I'VE MADE.

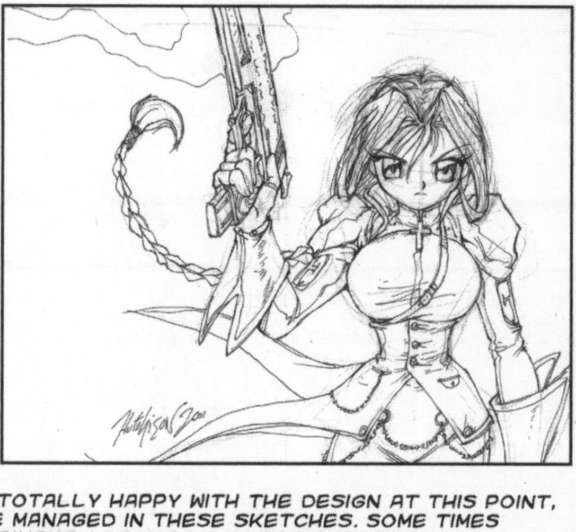

EVEN THOUGH I'M NOT TOTALLY HAPPY WITH THE DESIGN AT THIS POINT, I LIKE THE FLAVOR I'VE MANAGED IN THESE SKETCHES. SOME TIMES YOU'LL NEED TO EXPERIMENT. I DECIDED TO KEEP EXPERIMENTING BECAUSE THE CHARACTER HAS A LOT OF POSSIBILITIES.

HOW TO DRAW MANGA

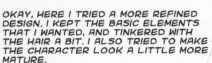

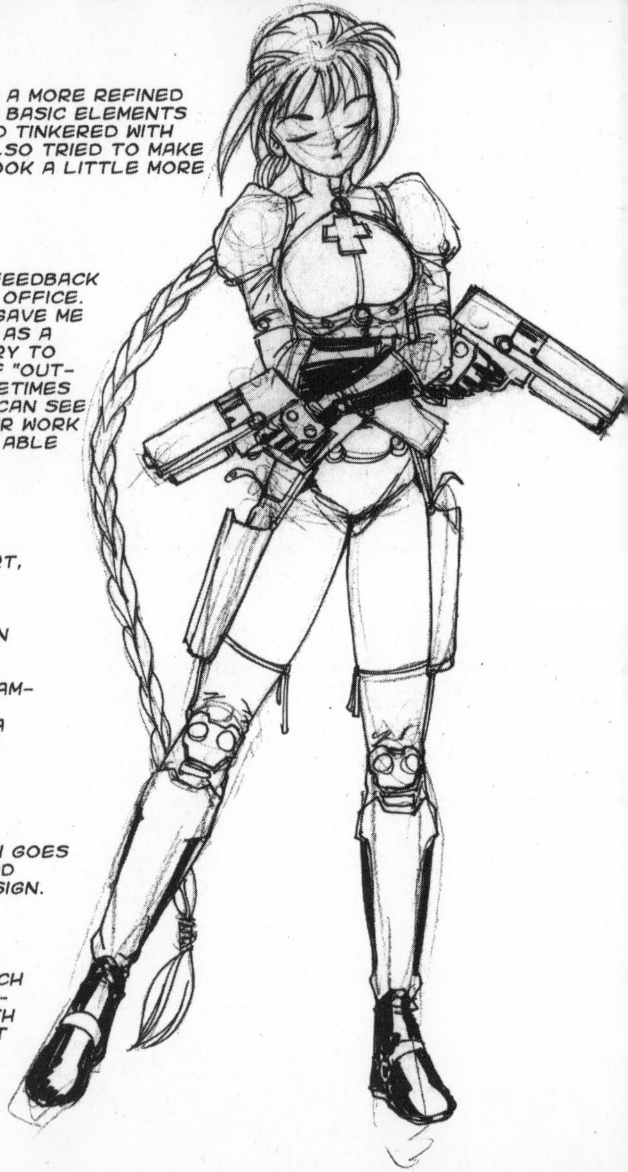

OKAY, HERE I TRIED A MORE REFINED DESIGN. I KEPT THE BASIC ELEMENTS THAT I WANTED, AND TINKERED WITH THE HAIR A BIT. I ALSO TRIED TO MAKE THE CHARACTER LOOK A LITTLE MORE MATURE.

I THEN GOT SOME FEEDBACK FROM AROUND THE OFFICE. GENERAL OFINION GAVE ME SOME NEW INSIGHT, AS A GENERAL RULE I TRY TO GET SOME SORT OF "OUT-SIDE" OPINION. SOMETIMES ANOTHER PERSON CAN SEE THINGS ABOUT YOUR WORK YOU MIGHT NOT BE ABLE TO RIGHT AWAY.

FOR THE MOST PART, PEOPLE THOUGHT THIS DESIGN GOT AWAY FROM THE ORIGINAL DIRECTION I HAD FOR THE CHARACTER. TOO MODERN AND STREAM-LINED. OVERALL THIS SKETCH HAS A KIND OF "SHOTGUN MARY" FEEL TO IT.

STILL, THIS SKETCH GOES A LONG WAY TOWARD FINALIZING THE DESIGN.

BY THE WAY, THIS IS THE FIRST SKETCH IN WHICH THE CHAR-ACTER. IS SEEN WITH HOLSTERS AS PART OF THE COSTUME.

WITH SOME FRESH INSIGHTS IN HAND, I WENT BACK TO THE DRAWING BOARD. I DECIDED TO GIVE THE OLDER DESIGN ANOTHER TRY. THIS TIME I DID A MORE REFINED PICTURE. MAYBE TECHNIQUE COULD HELP?

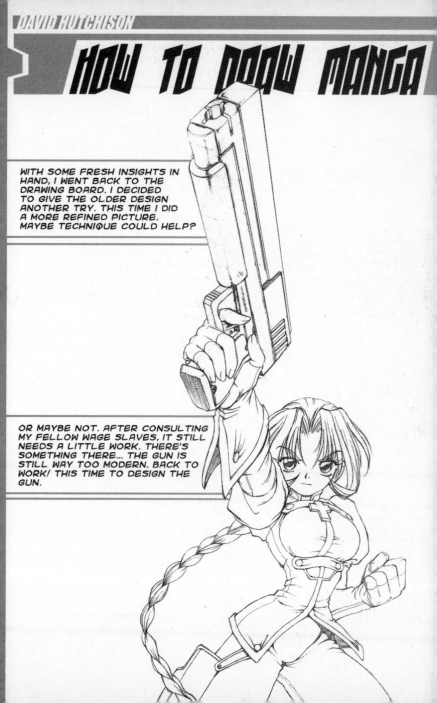

OR MAYBE NOT. AFTER CONSULTING MY FELLOW WAGE SLAVES, IT STILL NEEDS A LITTLE WORK. THERE'S SOMETHING THERE... THE GUN IS STILL WAY TOO MODERN. BACK TO WORK! THIS TIME TO DESIGN THE GUN.

SOMETIMES, I'M BAFFLED BY MY OWN THOUGHT PROCESS. YOU'LL OFTEN HEAR ME SAYING, "WHAT WAS I THINKING!". THIS WEAPON IS INSPIRED BY... TRIGUN MORE THAN ANYTHING, I GUESS. THERE CAN BE NO EXCUSE, THIS GUN IS NOT GOOD.

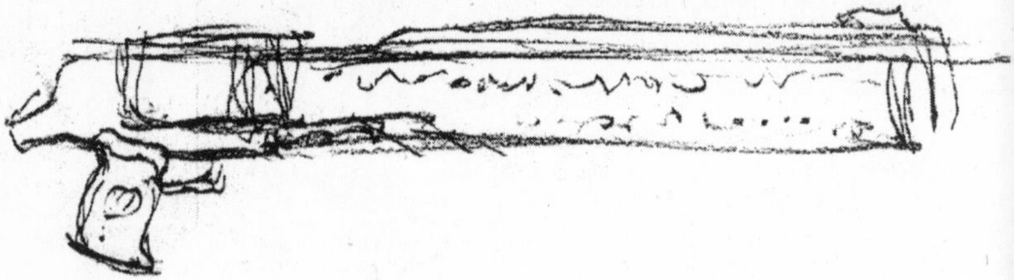

LUCKILY, A GOOD FRIEND LET ME BORROW A GUN REFERENCE BOOK FROM HIM. THE SAME DAY, I CAME UP WITH THIS...

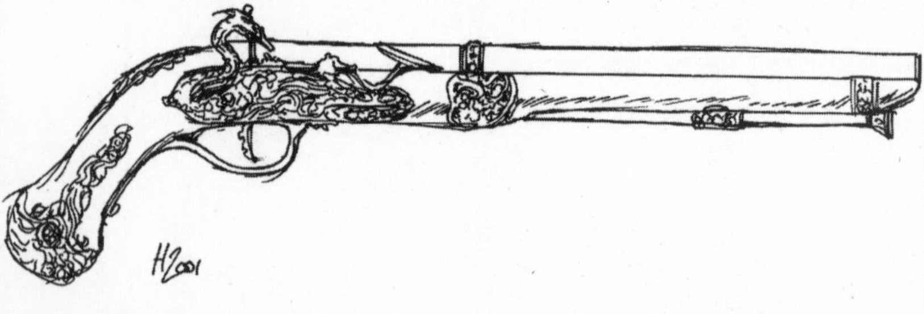

MUCH BETTER. AT THIS POINT. I THINK I'VE HIT ON SOMETHING! I LIKE THE ENGRAVING ON THE GUN SO MUCH, I'LL TRY TO INCORPORATE IT INTO THE CHARACTER DESIGN.

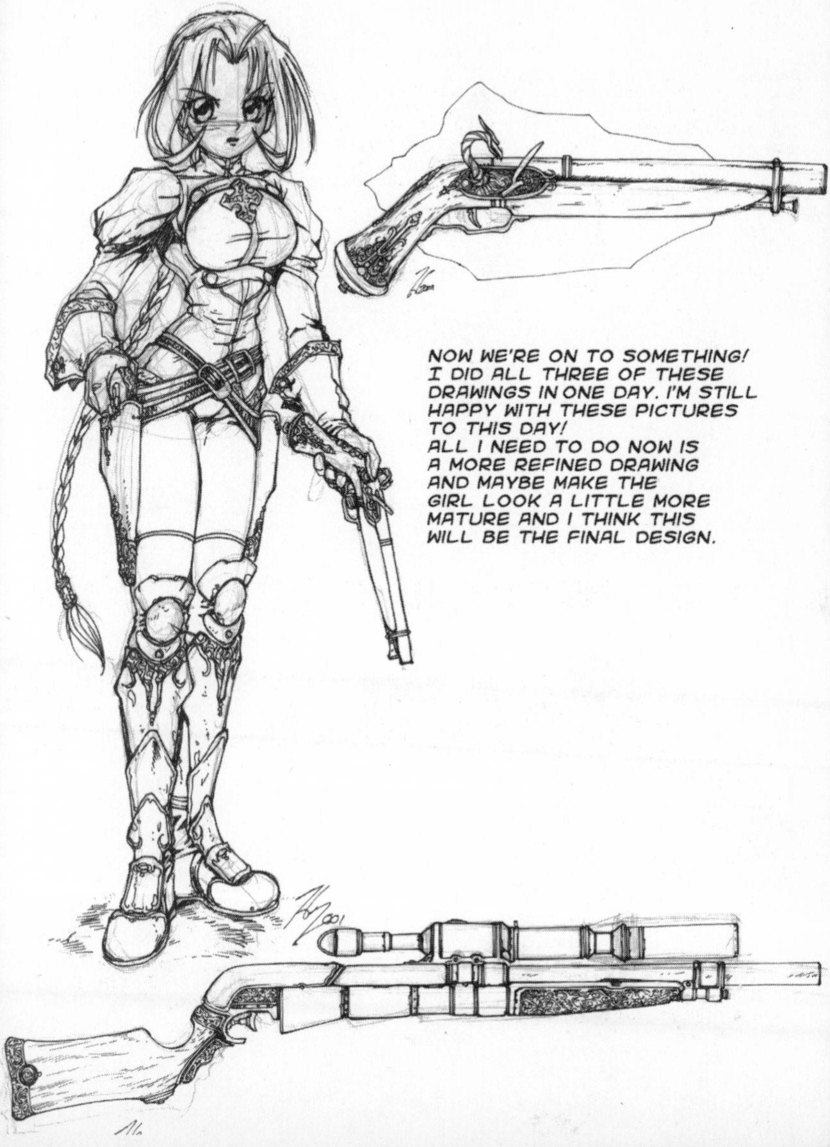

NOW WE'RE ON TO SOMETHING! I DID ALL THREE OF THESE DRAWINGS IN ONE DAY. I'M STILL HAPPY WITH THESE PICTURES TO THIS DAY!
ALL I NEED TO DO NOW IS A MORE REFINED DRAWING AND MAYBE MAKE THE GIRL LOOK A LITTLE MORE MATURE AND I THINK THIS WILL BE THE FINAL DESIGN.

WHEN I DREW THIS SKETCH, I KNEW THAT THE DESIGN PROCESS WAS DONE FOR THIS CHARACTER. NOW ALL I HAVE TO DO IS INK IT!

HOW TO DRAW MANGA

HERE'S THE FINAL PIECE. DESIGNING ANYTHING CAN BE REALLY EASY. OR IT CAN BE LONG AND DIFFICULT. BUT, BELIEVE ME, IT IS WORTH IT TO TRY. YOUR CHARACTERS HAVE TO LOOK LIKE THEY BELONG IN THE WORLDS YOU CREATE FOR THEM. PEOPLE WILL APPRECIATE THE EFFORT!

OH, 'TIS!
HERE'S THE FINAL RENDERING IN GRAYSCALE!
"MASTERFULLY" UTILIZED AS THE COVER FOR
HOW TO DRAW MANGA ISSUE 12! I'M SO PROUD!

PRACTICE PAGE

HOW TO DRAW MANGA

IN THIS SEGMENT, I'LL SHOW YOU HOW TO MAKE A QUICK-DESIGN CHARACTER. A QUICK-DESIGN CHARACTER CONSISTS OF A PROTOTYPE BODY AND A NUMBER OF DIFFERENT PROPS AND CLOTHING DESIGNS. IT'S KIND OF LIKE A PAPER DOLL, REALLY...

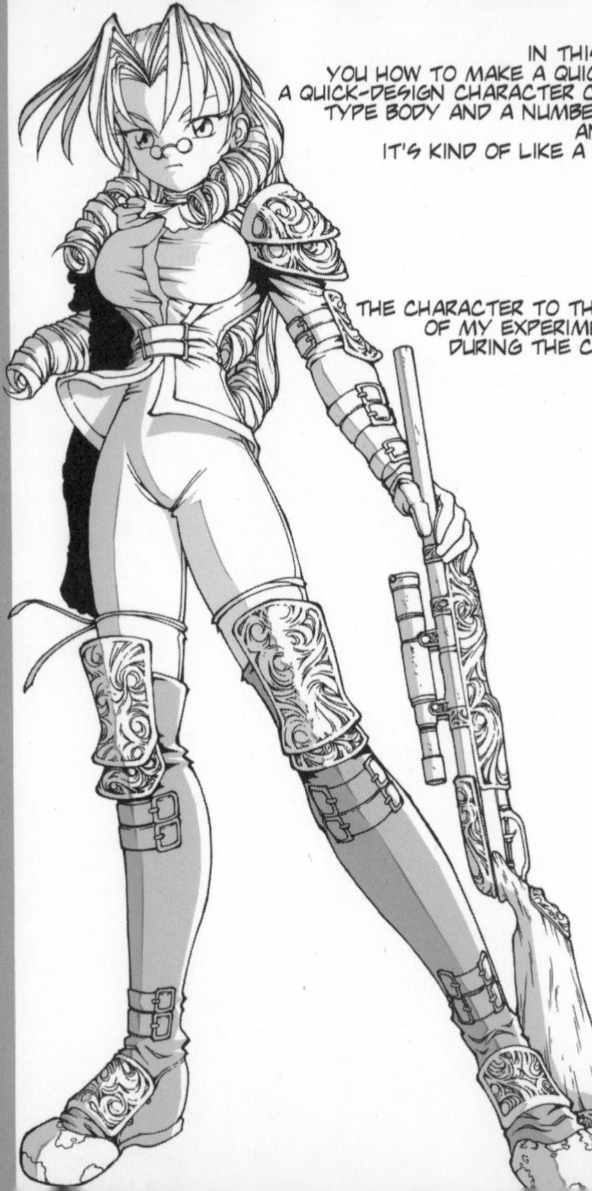

THE CHARACTER TO THE LEFT IS THE RESULT OF MY EXPERIMENTS IN QUICK DESIGN DURING THE CREATIVE PROCESS FOR ANOTHER CHARACTER.

DAVID HUTCHISON

HOW TO DRAW MANGA

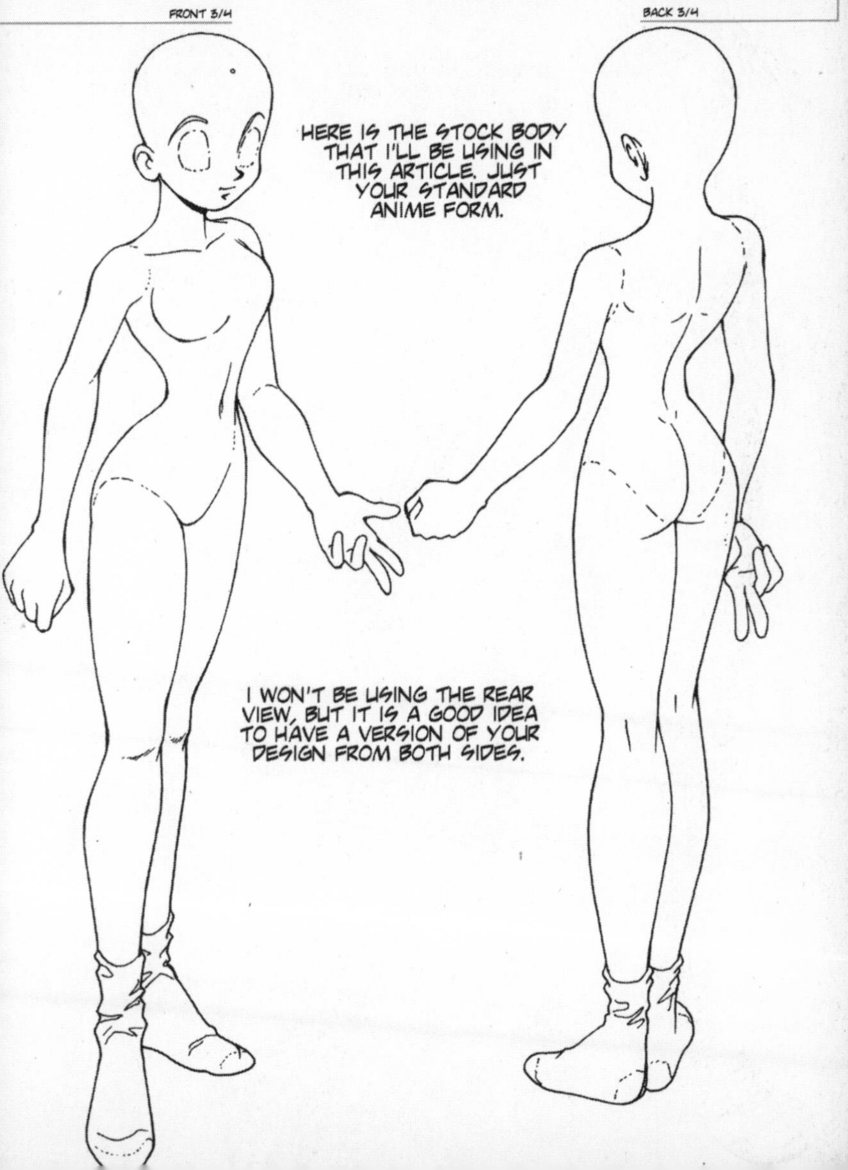

FRONT 3/4
BACK 3/4
HERE IS THE STOCK BODY THAT I'LL BE USING IN THIS ARTICLE. JUST YOUR STANDARD ANIME FORM.
I WON'T BE USING THE REAR VIEW, BUT IT IS A GOOD IDEA TO HAVE A VERSION OF YOUR DESIGN FROM BOTH SIDES.

HAIR

SKIRT/PANTS

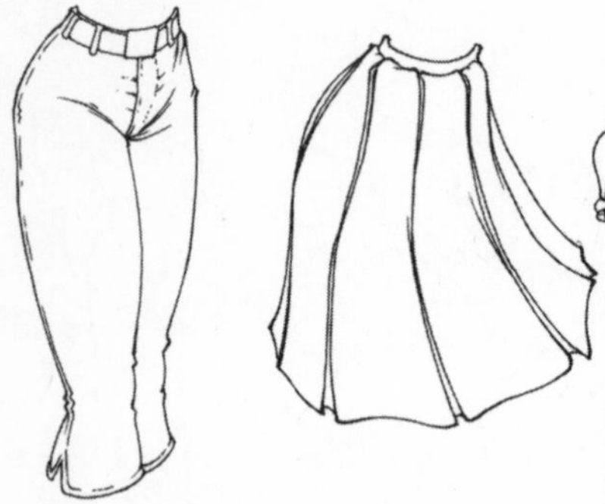

SHIRTS

ONCE YOU HAVE YOUR BODY AND YOUR PROPS ARE READY, YOU CAN QUICK-DESIGN TO YOUR HEART'S CONTENT!

SHOES

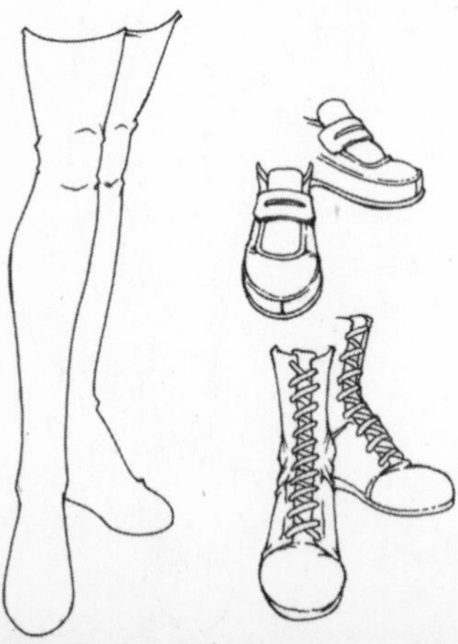

PROPS

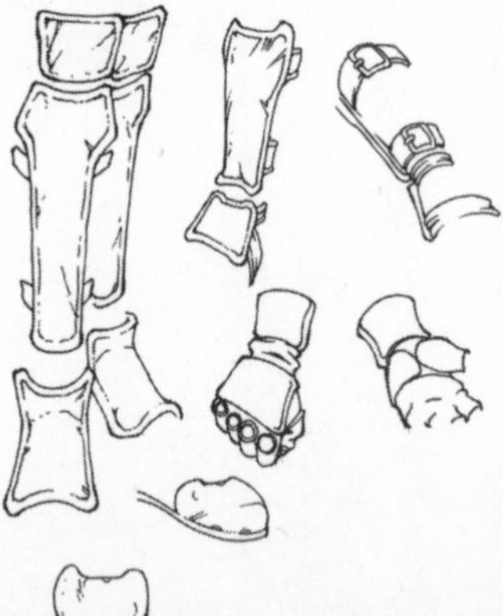

HEAD VARIATIONS

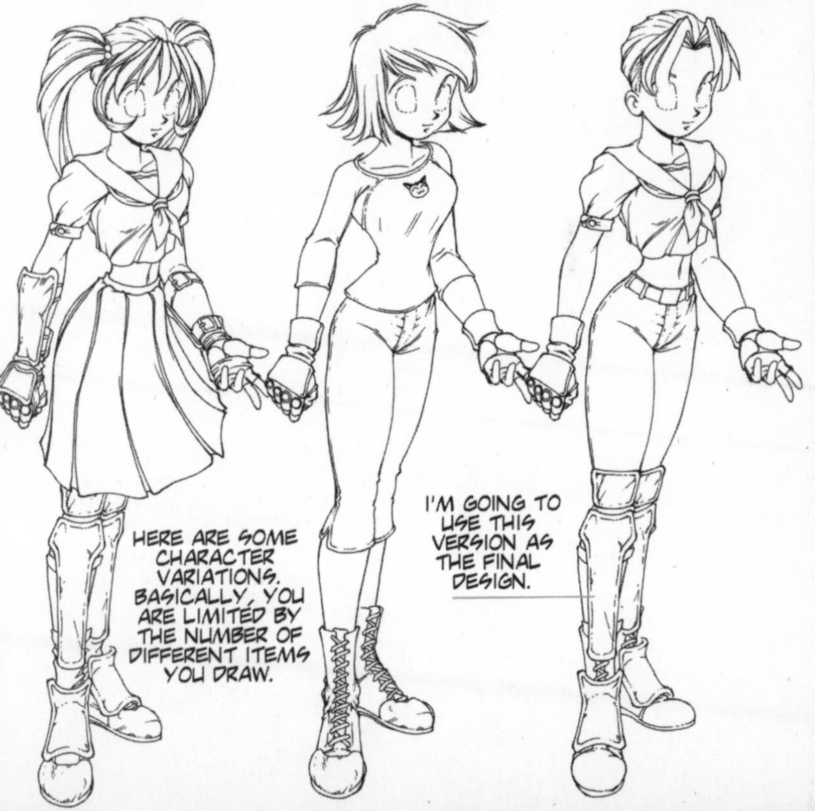

HERE ARE SOME CHARACTER VARIATIONS. BASICALLY, YOU ARE LIMITED BY THE NUMBER OF DIFFERENT ITEMS YOU DRAW.
I'M GOING TO USE THIS VERSION AS THE FINAL DESIGN.

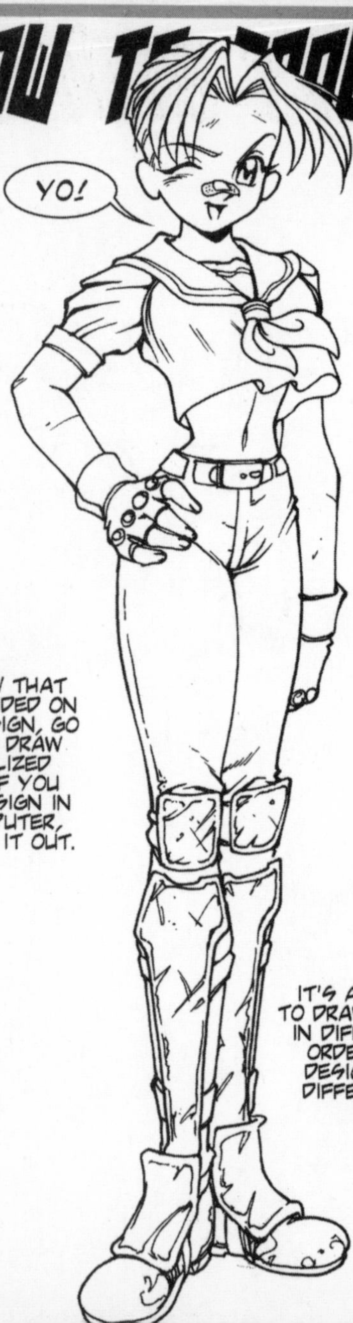

OKAY! NOW THAT YOU'VE DECIDED ON A FINAL DESIGN, GO AHEAD AND DRAW THE FINALIZED VERSION. IF YOU DID THE DESIGN IN THE COMPUTER, JUST PRINT IT OUT.

IT'S ALSO A GOOD IDEA TO DRAW YOUR CHARACTER IN DIFFERENT POSES IN ORDER TO SEE IF THE DESIGN WORKS FROM DIFFERENT VIEWS AND POSITIONS.

DRAWING THESE POSES IS ALSO IMPORTANT SO THAT YOU YOU CAN GET THE "FEEL" OF YOUR CHARACTER AND BECOME COMFORTABLE WITH DRAWING IT.

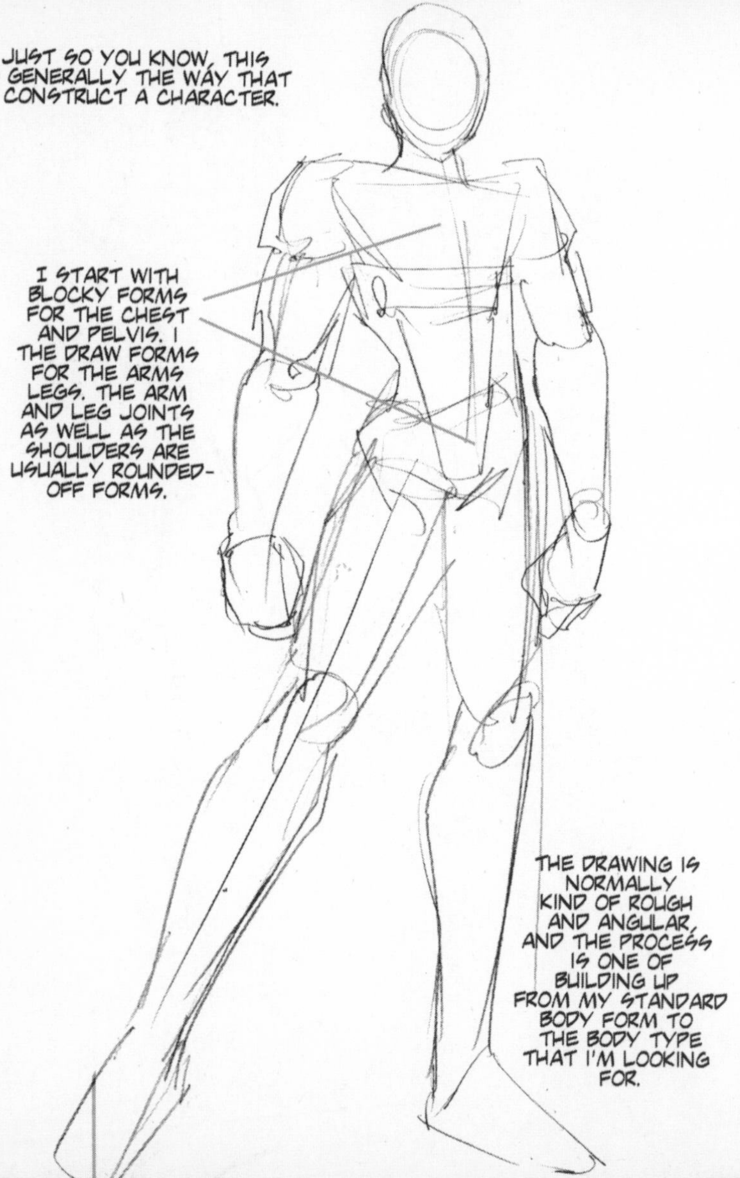
JUST SO YOU KNOW, THIS IS GENERALLY THE WAY THAT I CONSTRUCT A CHARACTER.
I START WITH BLOCKY FORMS FOR THE CHEST AND PELVIS. I THE DRAW FORMS FOR THE ARMS LEGS. THE ARM AND LEG JOINTS AS WELL AS THE SHOULDERS ARE USUALLY ROUNDED-OFF FORMS.
THE DRAWING IS NORMALLY KIND OF ROUGH AND ANGULAR, AND THE PROCESS IS ONE OF BUILDING UP FROM MY STANDARD BODY FORM TO THE BODY TYPE THAT I'M LOOKING FOR.

HERE'S THE REFINED SKETCH. WELL, I HOPE YOU FOUND THIS SECTION INTERESTING, AND I HOPE YOU USE SOME OF THESE IDEAS IN YOUR OWN WORK.

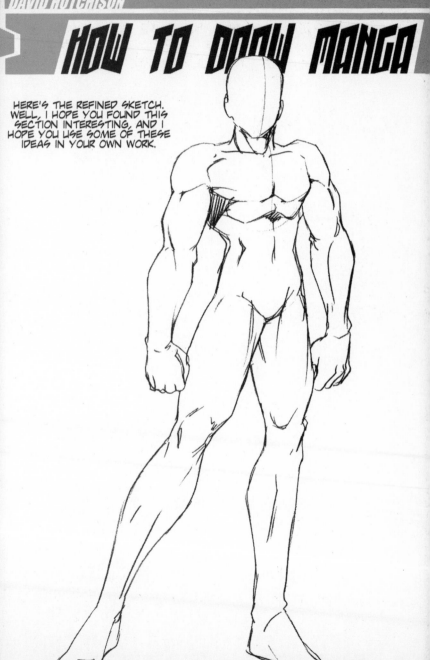

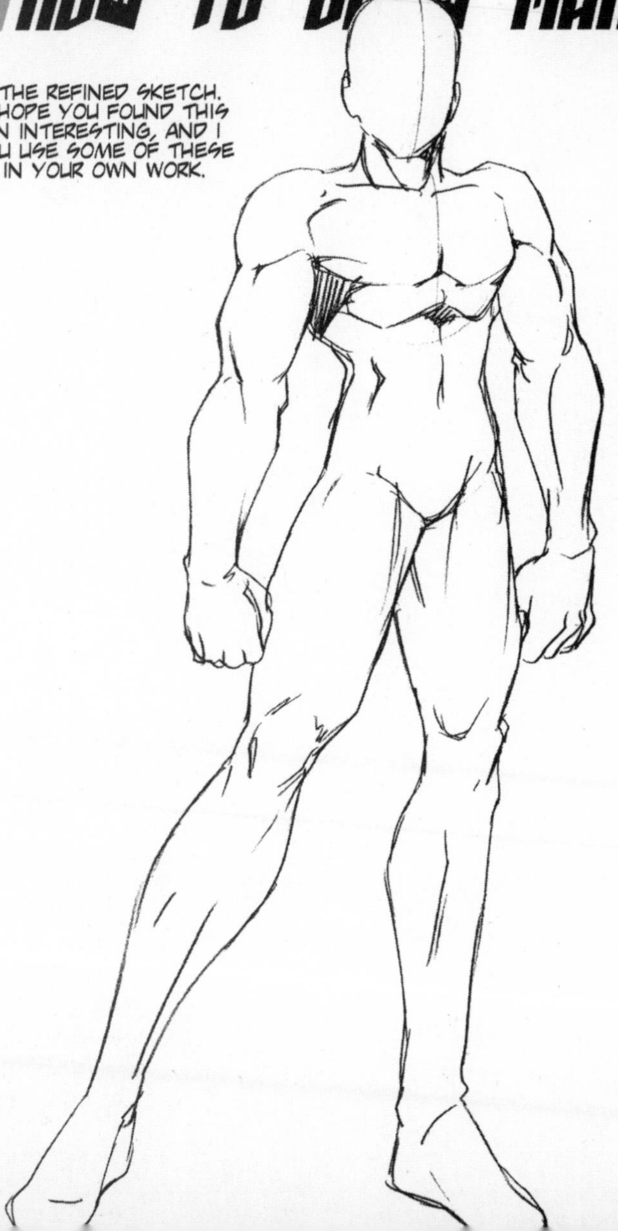

PRACTICE PAGE

I thought I'd cover some aircraft this time out and show you how I approach drawing planes. First up is an American Volunteer Group P-40 fighter. The P-40 ("P" for "Pursuit") was the first American fighter to officially score kills on Sunday morning, Dec. 7, 1941. The AVG, American pilots hired by the Chinese government, fought the Japanese over the skies of China under the direction of Gen. Claire Chennault. This example was cobbled together using many, many photos as reference (one for shape, one for details, one for markings, etc.).

P-40B TOMAHAWK

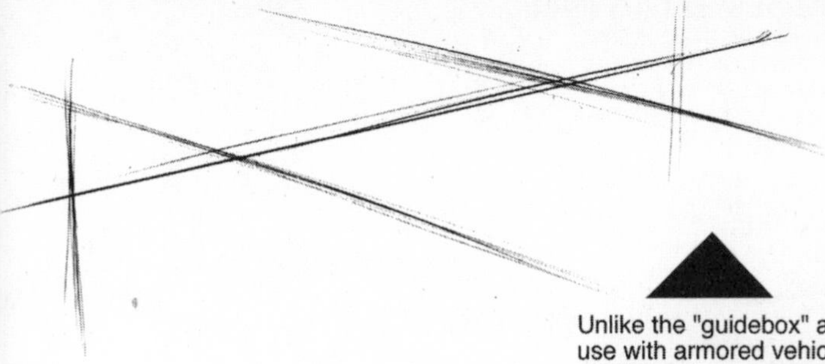

Unlike the "guidebox" approach I use with armored vehicles, I use a small set of perspective lines when drawing aircraft. They are, essentially, X,Y, and Z axis. On this plane (and the Tomcat later in this article), these axes help me wrap my head around where the plane will be. Since I'm looking at a photo, I generally don't adhere to these lines for perspective. The photo has done the perspective work for me, I just need to be aware of SHAPE and PROPORTION.

Next we start the fuselage. I usually start with the cockpit. Once I get that shape established, I can base the rest of the plane's proportions on it's shape and size. Notice all the vertical lines running down the fuselage. Some are actual aircraft panels that will be inked, some are just lines of reference I'm using to judge where, say, the wing attaches to the body. Also note the very shallow airscoop lines, later corrected as I established other proportions.

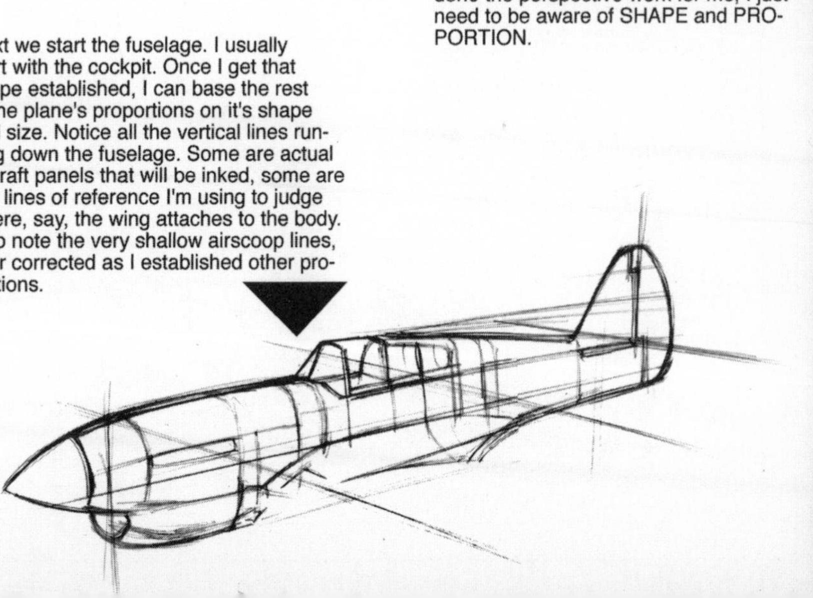

P-40B TOMAHAWK

The wing stage. I had trouble with this, I ignored my own advice and tried to use my perspective lines. Once I went back to trusting the photo, I faired better. This is a good stage to view your drawing back-wards in a mirror or up to the light (I know I say that in all my tutorials, but I can't stress this habit enough). Seeing the drawing backwards will show any flaws with your basic premise, and may help you spot things that don't look right to you, but you can't quite figure out why.

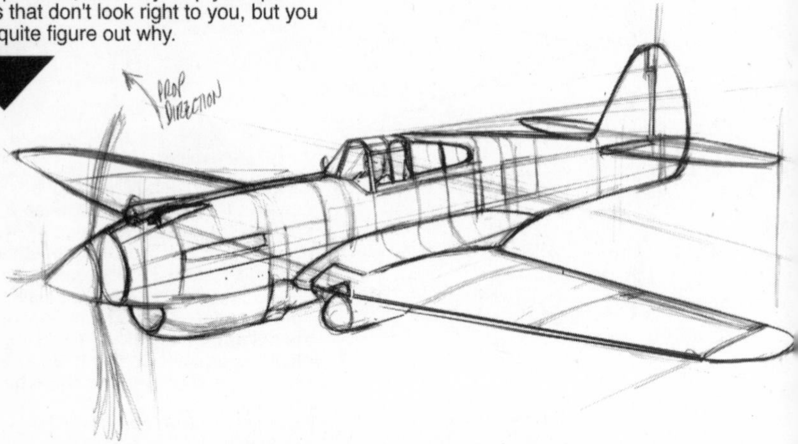

Here we are at "detail up", preparing for ink. The photo didn't show much panel detail, so I reffed a schematic for the wing panels. Also, my main photo wasn't in AVG livery, so I looked at several other pictures to place the shark's mouth and other markings.

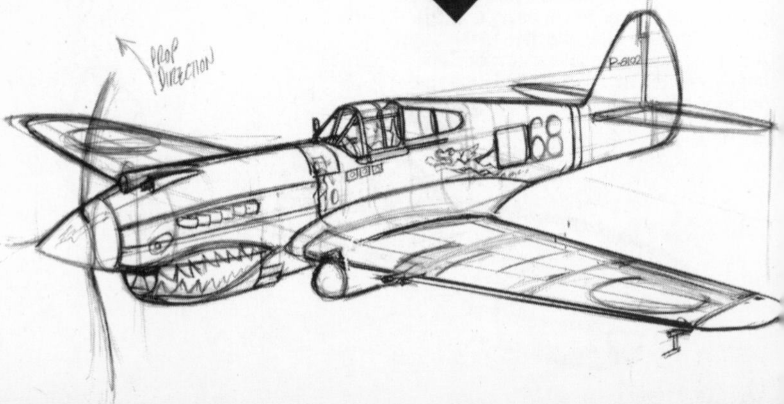

P-40B TOMAHAWK

Basic ink here. No line weight or variation. I could have used a straight edge for some of the wing panels, but I think a little imperfection can sometimes lend character to the art. Also here is where I've indicated a few scuffs and dings, trying to avoid a sterile, technical feel even more.

The P-40 with tones and markings. I followed the lighting from my main photo, I liked the satin highlights off the spinner and nose. I use Photoshop these days, but the same look can be achieved with markers and white chalk or pastel (maybe with more artistic results!) Did I mention I miss the markers? Ah, well, it's all going the way of the computer these days. One BIG advantage with using the machine is the opportunity to experiment instantly, without taking the risk of screwing up your original. Notice the paint chipped off and the exhaust stains.

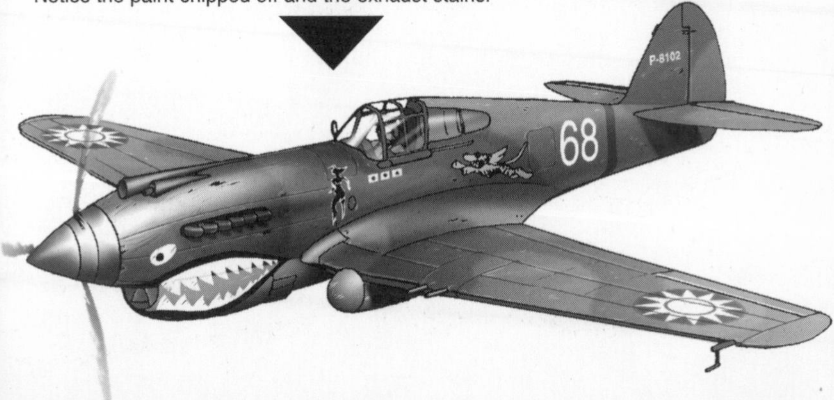

PRACTICE PAGE

Some fast clouds painted in Photoshop using the "wet edge" option on the paintbrush (at around 20 percent opacity). I ran a slight "Spatter" filter on some of it, and used the "Smudge" tool on a couple of places, dragging black into white and vice-versa, until I had some passable clouds that wouldn't fight with the focus of the piece.

Obviously, it's not necessary to throw this much attention to detail on every panel of your comic, but this would be a good **establishing shot**, or **page focus** (How to Draw Manga #5). This piece took about a day to complete. It might have taken a little less time if I didn't have to draw and scan each step, but still, a panel a day is way too slow for a comic book schedule. Choose your battles, too much detail is sometimes distracting, and when you DO spend time on a "money shot", it'll have that much more impact!

Remember to consider DISTANCE and DETAIL when toning/coloring (and inking for that matter). I have schematics of the P-40 that show rivet placement, serial number location, etc., but from this distance, it would be ridiculous, unrealistic (and time consuming) to render details to the Nth degree. DISTANCE from your subject will determine DETAIL.

A more dramatic, comic-style background. Same fighter, but I hit it with a 2 pixel "Median" filter to soften the sharper details. Median is one of my favorite filters. It blends without blurring.

This particluar P-40 was flown by Chuck Older, 3rd Squadron, "Hell's Angels", American Volunteer Group, based in Kunming, China in the spring of 1942. The AVG, also known as the "Flying Tigers", destroyed 229 enemy aircraft and lost 12 of their own. Chuck Older's fighter (no. 68) was recently found at the bottom of a lake in Kunming. It is the only remaining Flying Tiger.

JETSAM

Here's a B-17 bomber I did as a teaser for a story called "The Fort". I scanned my sketch and painted over it. As I worked on it, I found that I really liked the rough feel of the piece, so I tried to match the computer tones to the pencil (even as far as leaving the bits of random marks leftover from the scan.

In this detail shot, you can see a lot of my techniques: "wet edge" brush shadows, "Smudge" tool, a few random selections of light and dark, small diameter brush with the "Dodge" tool.

Here are a couple examples of full paint, no ink lines left. I sketched the aircraft, but it's unlikely I actually inked them, as they were just guidelines for the "Selection" tool and the "Paintbrush" tool. The Sabre jets (left) are, in fact, the same plane copied and altered slightly. I changed the plane numbers on the fuselages, and lit each one a little differently. The Panther jet (right) was pretty straightforward, almost all black. I think what really makes this piece is the dramatic backlighting. It helped that I had a definite idea for both of these pieces. I'm not 100 percent satisfied with the outcome (I never will be), but I think I was hitting on ten out of twelve cylinders on all three of these pieces (and, almost as importantly, I met the deadlines!).

WIGHT

Our second plane is the Grumman F-14 "Tomcat", the U.S. Navy's Fleet Defender. The Tomcat is a tough one to draw; there are few landmarks that are consistent through the fuselage, and the variable swing-wing feature can present big perspective problems. Also, the F-14 has lots of curved surfaces and dramatic angles on its wings. I relied heavily on the photo to make sure the SHAPES were looking right, no matter how much my mind told me to use perspective rules. I had a similar problem when I was drawing lots of Huey helicopters for Twilight X. I drew lots of Hueys looking at photo ref, and. it eventually got me familiar with the chopper's distinctive shapes. Now I can draw Hueys in my sleep. The Tomcat is another aircraft that requires photo ref at first to nail down its complicated shapes and angles. (I'm still working on it.)

F-14D TOMCAT

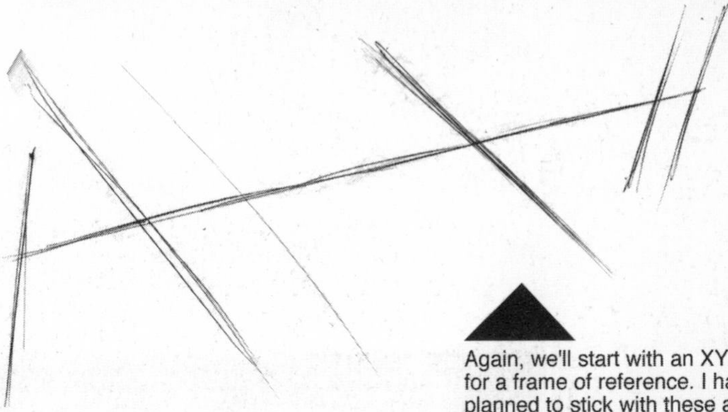

Again, we'll start with an XYZ axis for a frame of reference. I hadn't planned to stick with these axes as close as I did, I think I just happened to get the angles just right to match up well with the photo.

The fuselage, engines, and tails. I started with the nose on this one, the canopy is blended more with the body here than with the P-40, so I treated the cockpit as a shape rather than as a reference for proportion. It was essential to get the wing root "gloves" and the tails the way I wanted them; they would determine the wing placement in the next step.

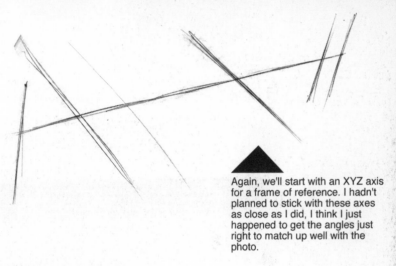

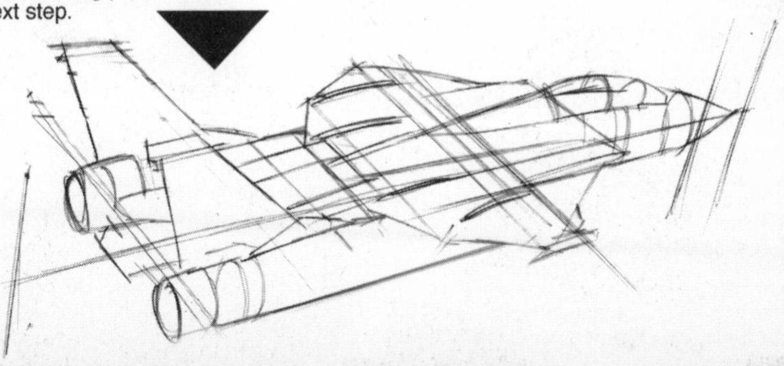

F-14D TOMCAT

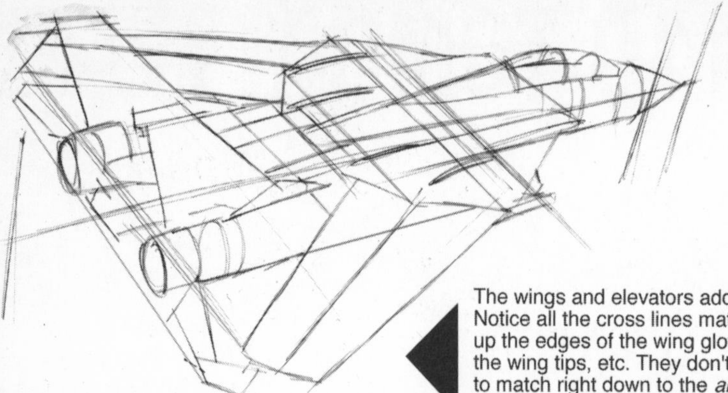

The wings and elevators added. Notice all the cross lines matching up the edges of the wing gloves, the wing tips, etc. They don't have to match right down to the *angstrom*, but they need to be pretty close.

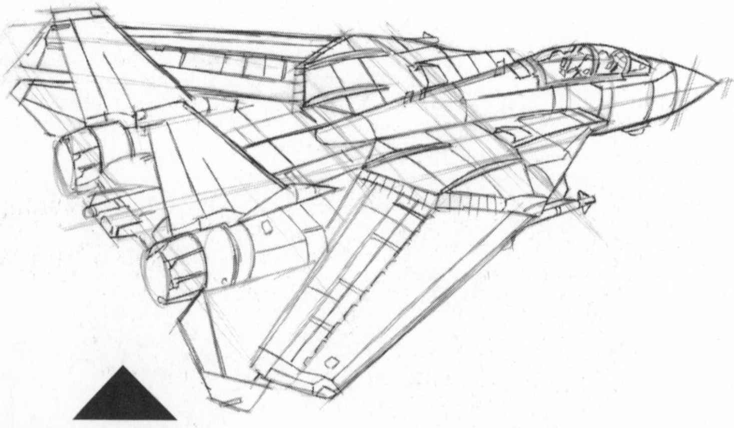

"Detail up" on the Tomcat. This took a while. I decided to add lots of panels and details on this one, I knew I could always remove details in Photoshop if I wanted to (turns out I didn't, but I DID make some panels less conspicuous on the final version).

F-14D TOMCAT

Ink final. There's a little bit of straight edge on the wings, but I tried to avoid the ruler as much as I could. Notice I left some of the engine exhaust area blank, in preparation for a dramatic afterburner effect. As it turned out, I could have inked the whole engine, as my effect was more subtle than I first envisioned.

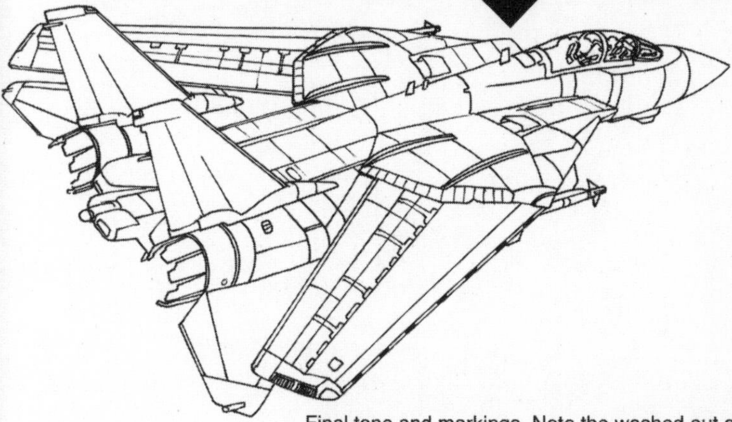

Final tone and markings. Note the washed out appearance of some of the wing and body panels. The black line ink was on a "layer" in Photoshop. I selected certain portions and hit them with the "Eraser" tool at about 60 percent, giving them a little less opacity. There's lots of "wet edge" brush work on some of the panels, and an overall grimy pattern of lighter and darker areas. Tomcats on the carrier get weathered and mottled, almost dingy (must be the salt air), but the paint doesn't seem to chip of like the old WW2 paint on the P-40, so there shouldn't be any sharp lines on your weathering here.

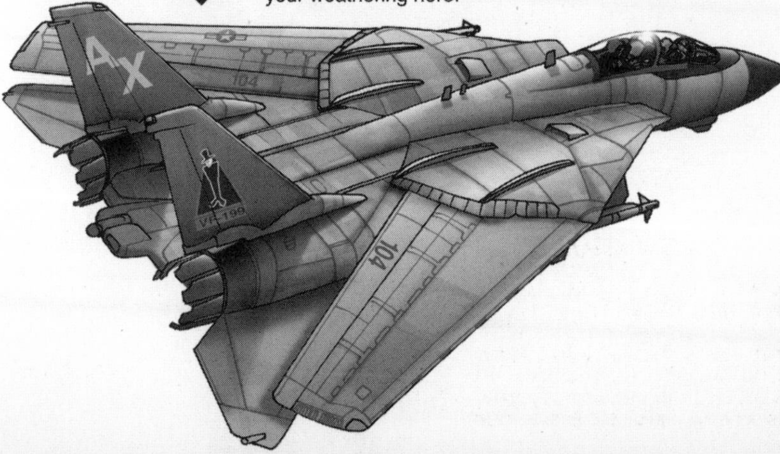

The Tomcat over water I'd originally painted for Twilight X: Episode One. I threw it in here, tweaked it a little, and decided to keep it. A logical, simple background that shows off the fighter. Perfect. I added the afterburners and blurred the background behind the jetwash.

Again, this fighter took me a full day from start to finish. For the sake of How to Draw Manga, I took the time to try and explain some of the tricks I use. This doesn't mean I use ALL of them ALL of the time. Don't try to knock every panel "out of the park". As you do more pages, some things will get easier (perspective, camera. etc.), and you'll be able to take the time to experiment without blowing your deadline.

Same fighter with a quick carrier deck and a 1 pixel "Median" filter. I try to save elements like this Tomcat as separate files in my machine. They might come in handy as background pieces.

PRACTICE PAGE

Our next project is the M3 CFV, a scout version of the Bradley Fighting Vehicle. Ideally, I would have a model or a toy of this rig to refer to, as it has more angles than Euclid! Boxes, curves, and asymmetrical slopes are the rule rather than the exception on this beast. I reffed a photo for this one and concentrated on the shapes from the photo, rather than trying to translate things into rules of perspective. There are many versions of this machine, all with slight but noticeable differences. If I were to feature this vehicle in a story where I had to draw it often, I'd DEFINITELY build a model or buy a toy of it. It's awfully complicated, and some parts of it were obscured in shadow on the pictures I had.

BRADLEY M3A1

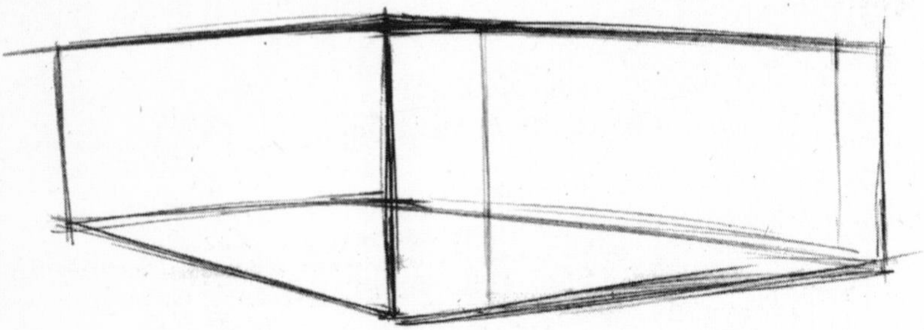

The box again, drawn here so we know where we are. Again, note the corner closest to us.

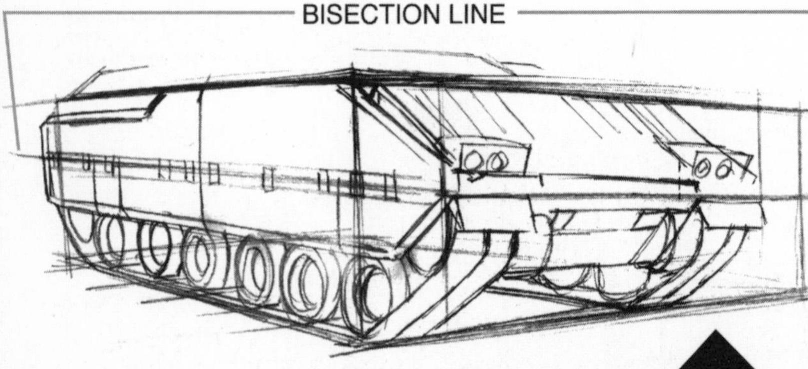

Here we've bisected the box horizontally. This split is one of the few "landmarks" we can work from, it cuts the upper and lower slopes of the nose, and it follows along the side skirts. I referred to the photo often, trying to keep the shape of the skirt in proportion with itself. See how we've tacked the nose to the face of the guidebox again.

BRADLEY M3A1

Here we've concentrated on the SHAPE of the upper hull and turret, looking at the photo constantly to make sure of the size and space they occupy. Here the front edge of the driver's hatch and the barrel of the 25mm cannon meet vertically. The upper hull is a complicated set of slopes and angles. The rough shapes of these are sketched in here.

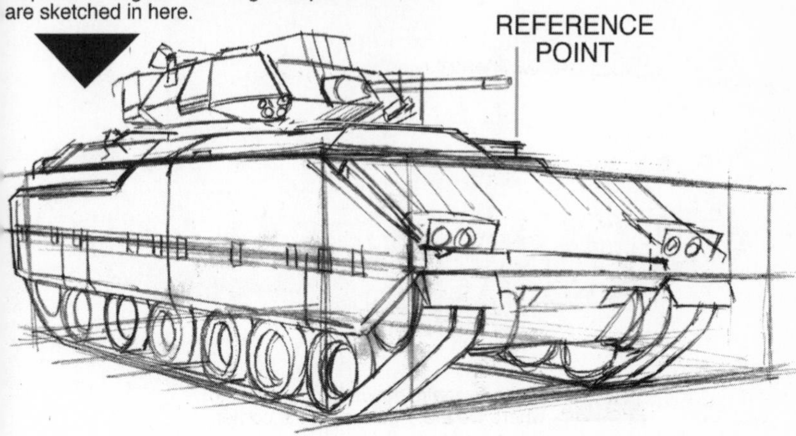

Here we are, tightening the pencils and adding detail. Much of this detail is just drawing a shape that matches the photo. Ideally, we would know exactly what we're drawing, but the photos have let us down. Shadows and highlights are all we're left with, so we've indicated them as best as we can.

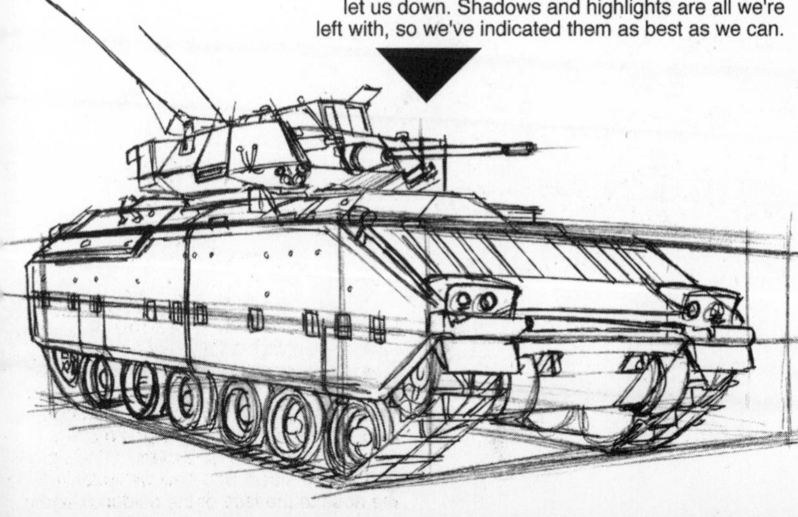

BRADLEY M3A1

Inks, looking deliberate, even though we're not sure about some of the details. Tones will save us; we can hide things in shadow.

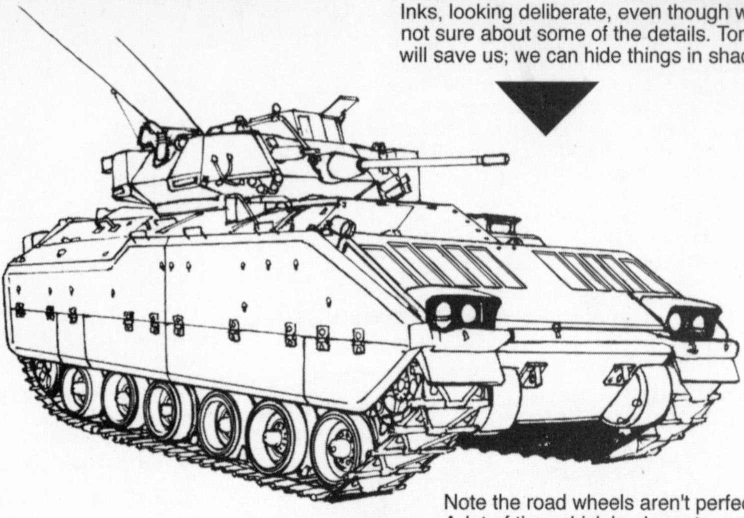

Note the road wheels aren't perfect. A lot of the vehicle's character can be indicated with rough road wheels. Remember, those wheels all have independent suspension, and they're sometimes replaced or in need of replacement. An irregular surface might push one or two wheels up higher than the rest.

And finally, tones and shading hiding a multitude of sins.

PRACTICE PAGE

A fast background that sets off the vehicle, and establishes an uncertain mood. A misty European morning, a partial blasted building, and a buttoned up rig says there might be trouble ahead. The fog in the foreground was done on a layer, so that I might experiment with just how much of the vehicle will be seen, and how much will be obscured.

A more dramatic weather experiment, leaving little doubt about the inclement atmosphere. Again, BRIGHTNESS/CONTRAST gave me the basic lighting for the vehicle. The BURN tool pushed the tail into the shadows, and the MOTION BLUR tool produced the rain. The headlight effect was achieved with a PAINTBRUSH set on DISSOLVE, then motion blurred.

JETSAM

An M3 in the snow, from "Twilight X: Holiday" (1994). Notice that back then I wasn't as obsessed with getting every rivet drawn in with precision and accuracy. I was more interested in getting a mood, a feeling across. I hope someday to find the perfect balance of technical accuracy and dramatic license.

These were rendered with pen and ink and grey markers. There's some white paint and white pastel to break up some of the grey edges. Note the lack of detail in the treads and wheels, this gives the piece has a sense of movement and power.

Let's move on...

ROD'S DRAWING FUN FACTORY

MUCH ADO ABOUT HANDS

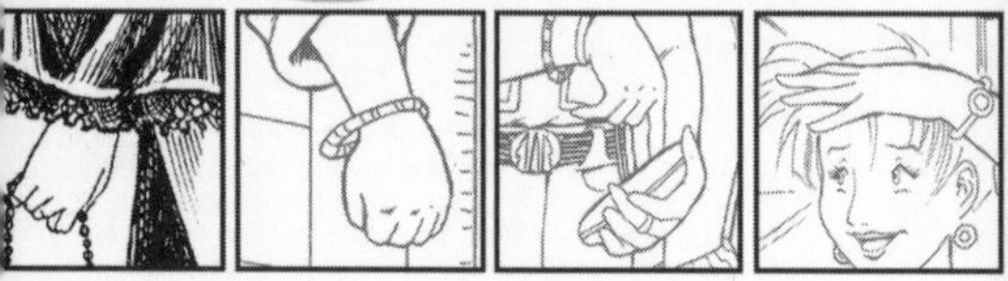

In this section, we will be tackling anatomy details normally not discussed in drawing books.

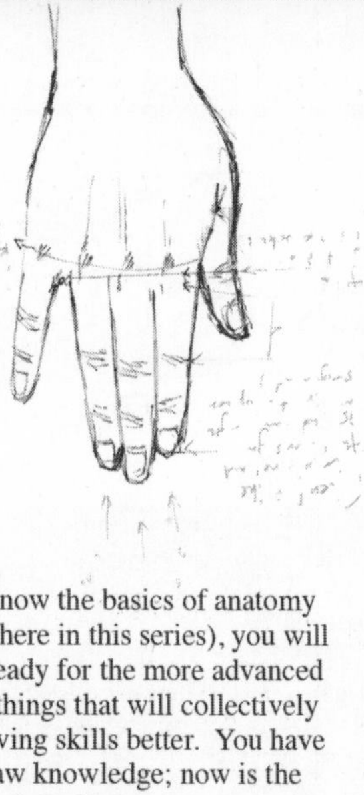

When you know the basics of anatomy (outlined elsewhere in this series), you will eventually be ready for the more advanced lessons—little things that will collectively make your drawing skills better. You have the skills and raw knowledge; now is the time to sharpen them further.

This time, we will be discussing hands.

We have plenty of influences around us. Over the years, we have copied off other artists -- including their mistakes Sure, you like how "Artist X" does his style. By all means, draw using his technique, but for crying out loud, don't copy his bad anatomy!!!

It is therefore my duty to help you make yourselves masters at your craft. Applied well, your knowledge and skill mixed with a lot of patience and perseverance, will catapult your skills to a level that will surpass even the favorite "superstar" artists of today.

Let us begin.

Additional notes about Hand Proportions...

For Advanced Learners... How to Draw" Good Hand
Anyone can draw hands... I assume you've also
learned the basics and are ready to move
Effective hands!

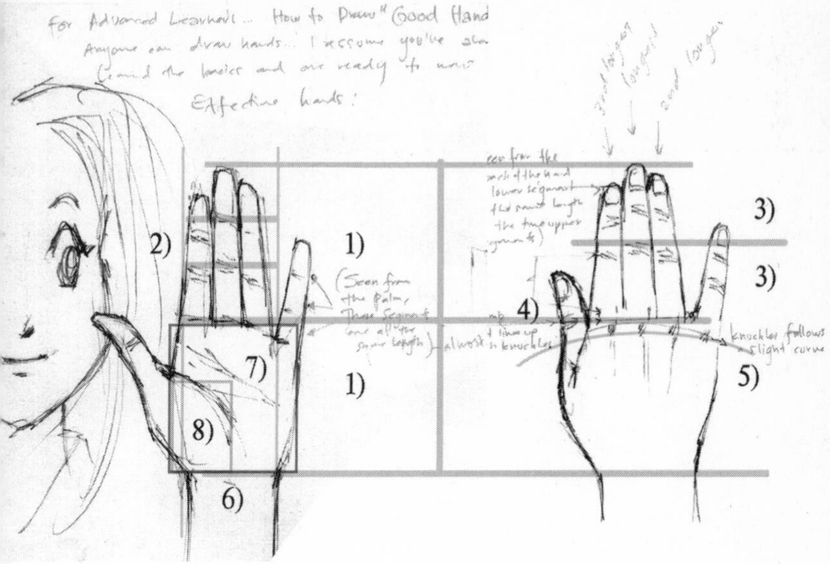

Some more proportions about hands you may or may not already know...
(You can look at your own hand.)

1) The length of the middle finger is approximately the same length as that of the palm from the base of the middle finger to the joint of the wrist.

2) Palm up, the three segments of each finger are all about the same length.

3) Viewed from the back of the hand, the distance from the knuckle to the first joint is equal to the length of the other two joints combined.

4) The thumb joint lines up with the knuckles.

5) The knuckles follow a slight curve.

6) The three middle fingers line up with the wrist when the hand is at rest.

7) Palm lines. Like thumbprints, no two are ever alike.

8) Thumb muscle occupies just a little over 1/4 of the palm.

PRACTICE PAGE

Hands Holding Weapons

Too many times, I have seen the same mistake over and over again; artists drawing their hands in balled fists and then adding a weapon handle at the sides to indicate a clutched weapon. It's been done so many times and by so many "superstars" that we end up imitating them.

Wrong!

This is not just about how to draw manga, this article is also all about how to draw correctly; accurately.

You will notice that even though I draw a lot of fists clutching weapons, each is held either tightly or loosely. Drawing tightly balled fists all the time eliminates your ability to express a lot of emotions.

Holding Weapons Right

In real life, hands do not close completely over the weapon handle. I don't care if it looks really "cool" to draw a closed fist over a handle, it simply isn't accurate to do so.
This is an example of my earlier drawings when I too, closed my fists around my weapon handles. IT looks cool, but it's hardly anatomically accurate.
I realized that the day I become satisfied with what I can draw is the day my skills will cease to improve...

This is an example of my earlier drawings when I too, closed my fists around my weapon handles.

Hands Holding Weapons (Action)

Examine Thealyn here, flailing her weapon. Again, the fist never really fully closes over the handle. An artist who has done his homework will also know that flailing weapons like these are not held tightly like crude clubs. Notice how lightly her left hand (yes, the hand to YOUR right...) holds her weapon - ready to let it fly in an instant.

Hands Holding Weapons

Another example of the quick-fingered warrior. This one's Gwennis. Hopefully, I'll be able to introduce her to you in my stories soon.
She's a happy-go-lucky free spirit. Because I rendered her loosely holding the daggers in an almost casual manner, can't you just imagine her bubbly personality?

What if I had drawn her with tight fists in this panel?

With just the way she holds the daggers, doesn't that give you a sense that she is an expert at flinging those things with a flick of her wrist?

Hands Holding Weapons

Let's take a look at Numo, here.
There are angles of course, where the fist will appear to engulf the weapon (A).
But check out how he holds the mace... That's one of the more difficult angles to execute which is why we don't see it very often.

Notice how proper perspective and anatomy combined play a vital role in making the illustration more interesting.

More on Holding Weapons

Here are more hand examples. There's a wide range of ways a hand can twist from the wrist. It is important to note the hand's maximum flexibility to avoid making the hands look broken.

Another thing to note is the angle of the thumb. When clutching objects like weapon handles, be careful how you position the thumb. Unless the character is holding the weapon in a vise-like grip, the thumb mostly crosses the fingers at an angle - very seldom perpendicular to the fingers.

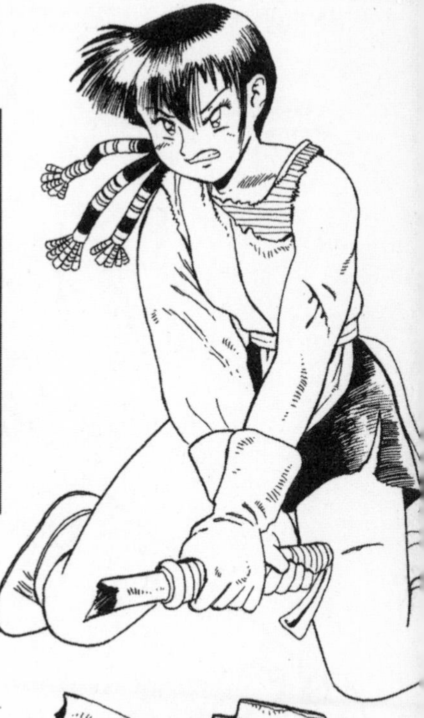

Here's a tense moment... Talis just broke her weapon and is quite mad... Grip is as tight as can be without losing accuracy...

See how the relaxed grip lends a more realistic touch on this illustration. While doing comics lends itself to much exaggeration, we must never forget the basic principles of proper drawing.

Hands Holding a Bow

It is often very difficult to draw an archer well. Hand positioning is everything. Ideally, the bow and arrow must form a perfect "T". This illustration is still far from accurate, though.

Can you spot the error?

The hand drawing the string ought to be turned palm up.

This is one instance where you can learn from MY mistakes...

More Hands or... No Hands

Sometimes, we cheat... but not always.
You know she is clutching a knife, but do you see her hand? In this instance, it is important that one gets the angle of the arm just right to express this or it will not work.
It's all part of the magic of art and illustration.

Check out the skeleton clutching the sword at the back...
This is probably one of those rare times it pays off to know basic bone structures.

Some basic hand types.

The "Dainty hand"
Archetype:
Feminine hands.
Delicate. Gentle.

The "Workman's hand"
Archetype:
Strong. Tough hero.
Capable. Brute.
Man's hands.

The "Bony Hand"
Archetype:
Shows age. Horror.
Vampire's hand.
Undead. Scary.
Claw like.

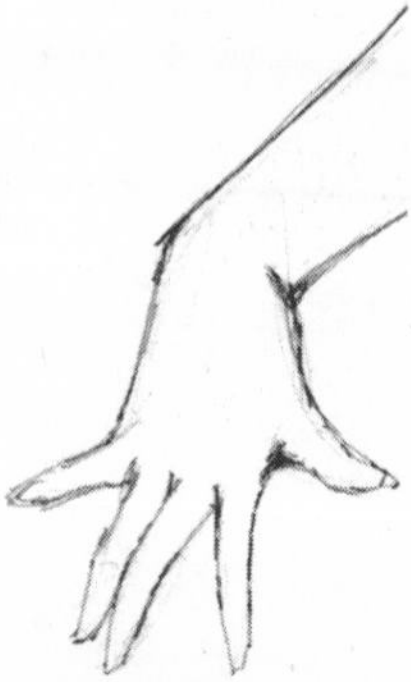

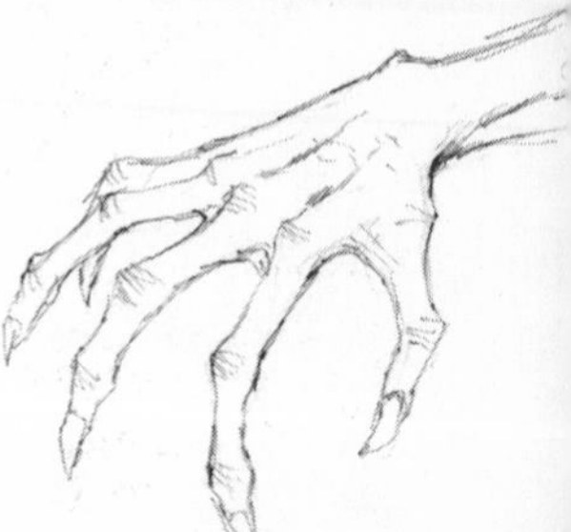

MUCH ADO ABOUT HANDS

Hands Holding Guns

Ah... Guns!!! What will our comics world do without them?

Again, the same tragic mistake most artists make is drawing a closed fist and then drawing a pistol over the hand... Be careful with that thumb... It's not drawn parallel to the handle.

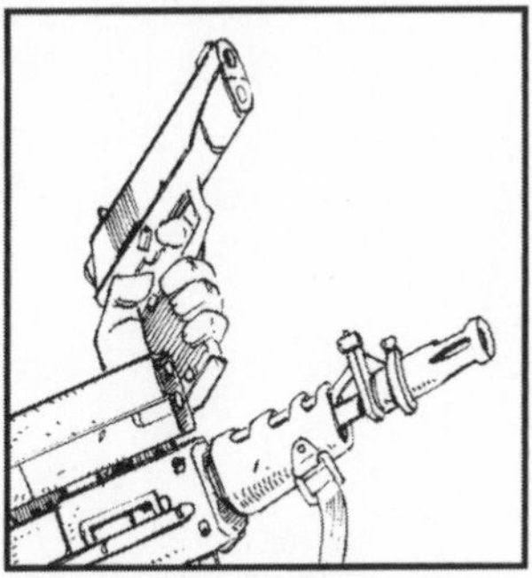

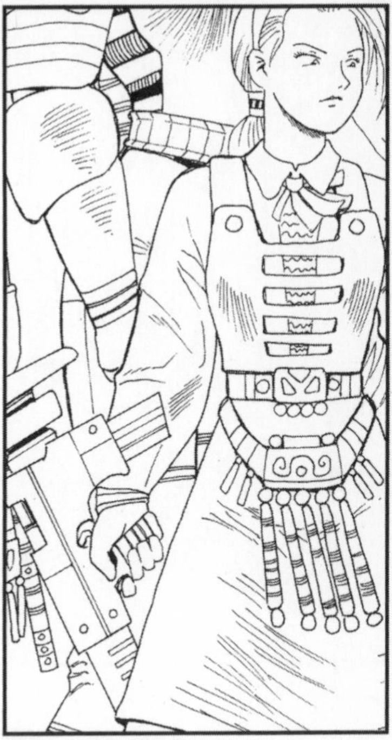

Go ahead... try holding a toy gun in your hand and see the difference...

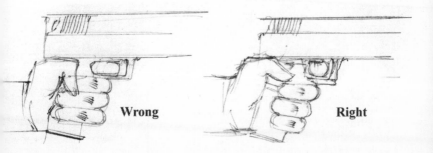

MUCH ADO ABOUT HANDS

Hands Holding Guns

Not so Correct...
Blood Gore's hand posture here is not really accurate...

Better...
Yunna's hand posture is better, don't you think?

So much can be done to enhance a story just by improving on how one places and poses hands.

Like real life, to be believable, comics characters need to have a wide range of expressions. It's details like these that will make your world come alive.

PRACTICE PAGE

MUCH ADO ABOUT HANDS

Enhancing the Mood

Does this picture not tell you that he is practicing at ease? Maybe at home? Unhurried. Relaxed, but stern and serious about his craft. It also speaks about his martial arts training.

If those were balled fists, the effect would not be the same. Perhaps some of you are familiar with the martial arts too. Some see the balled fist as the brute's weapon; a cultured warrior hardly has to resort to such things, thus the open palm and the eagle claw - symbols of higher training than just punching your way through sand bags.

I have nothing against balled fists. If I got to use them, I"ll use them... But it is easily one of the most overused elements in comics storytelling. The point of this series is to show you that there is much more - so much more to hands than just for waving and hitting faces with.

MUCH ADO ABOUT HANDS

Hands Enhancing Expressions

Hands are one of the human body's most expressive parts. If done right, you can express a wide range of emotions and feeling with just the way you place and position hands.

Here is the same shot -- this time, note how Yunna's other arm goes around the body of Mogka...

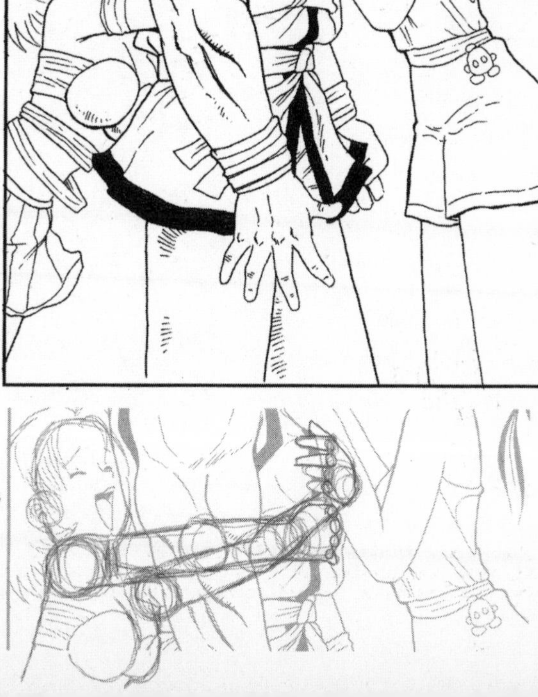

MUCH ADO ABOUT HANDS

Enhancing the Mood

Well, characters can't always be fighting and angry, can they? Well, at least not in my world... There is so much that can be done that isn't done, which is why I enjoy myself whenever I illustrate the more mundane aspects of the stories I write.

Hands can be put to a myriad of gestures and positions. Take a look at Travie below playing the guitar...

"But... what good does knowing how to draw a man plucking guitar strings do?"

Remember that comics is storytelling. Your characters will depend largely on how much life you give them. Sometimes drawing them doing mundane things makes them special. It makes them real to your reader.

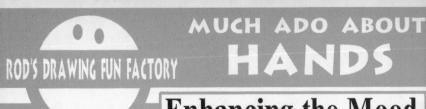

Looks like Ayinama released something nasty! See how her hands cradle the tiny box.

ROD'S DRAWING FUN FACTORY

MUCH ADO ABOUT HANDS

Enhancing the Mood

Compare these two scenes.
Which is the better, hotter scene?
This one?

Or this one?

PRACTICE PAGE

The future looks good...

We cannot avoid drawing hands all our lives. They cannot be in pockets or behind characters' backs in all our panels. Believe me, I've tried... When I realized I must learn more, I took every lesson to heart and practiced a lot.

We can exaggerate and stylize, but the important thing is that we learn the rules first, before we start breaking them.

The good news is that there are more and more of you out there who approach us every year at conventions or mail their stuff in. A lot of you have talent - more potential than you'll ever know. All it needs is some cutting and polishing so keep practicing a lot.

The contours of shoes and socks also follow the shape of the feet. Below are some diagrams detailing how the underlying shape of the foot affect clothing and footwear.

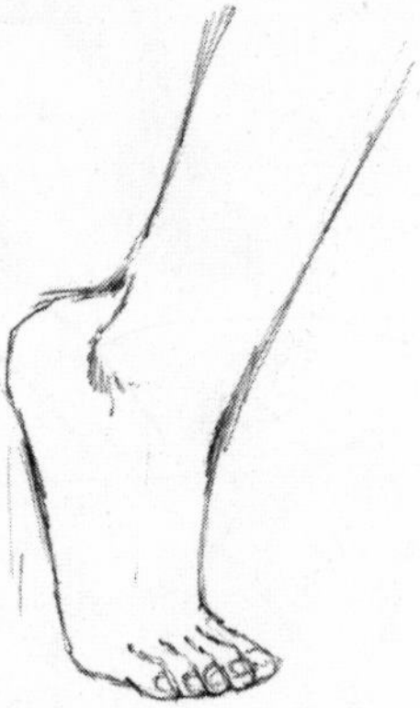

The shoes follow the contours of the foot. Studying the basic structure of the foot well helps in drawing shoes, boots and other footwear better.

Bare feet can sometimes add sizzle to your pin-up girls...

Breaking the foot down into basic shapes helps too.

As always, a good working knowledge in basic anatomy helps in drawing even the wierdest of shoe wear. Somehow, the shoe or boot always follows the contour of the foot.

Too Little

Too much

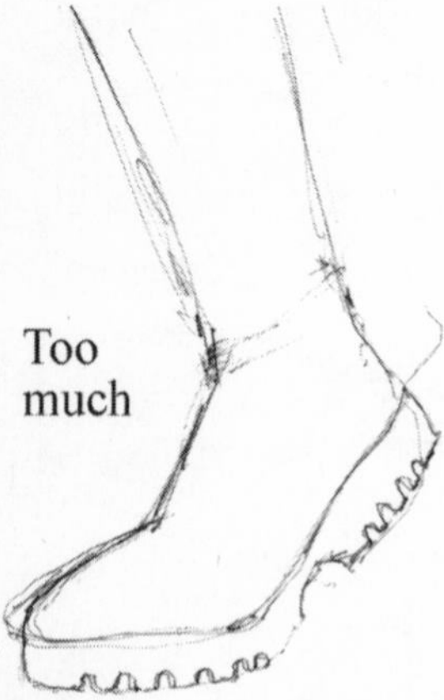

Just Right

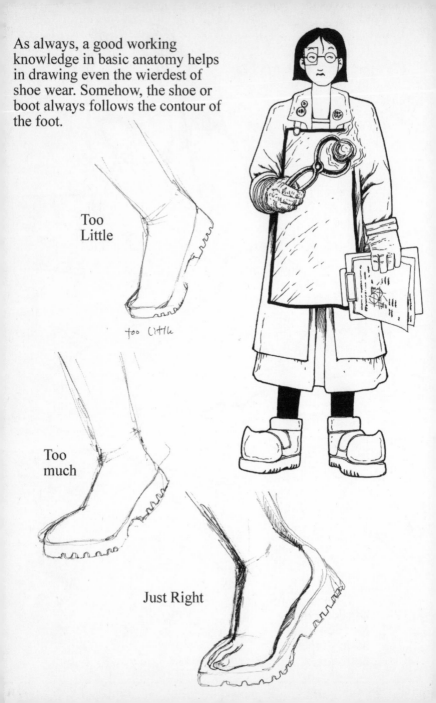

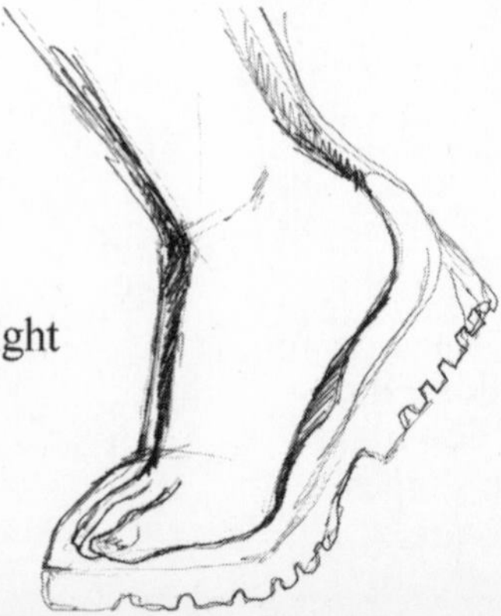

PRACTICE PAGE

If the shoe
fits...

It takes lots
of practice to
get things right.
But you will find
it easier each time
you try as long
as you put your will
into it.

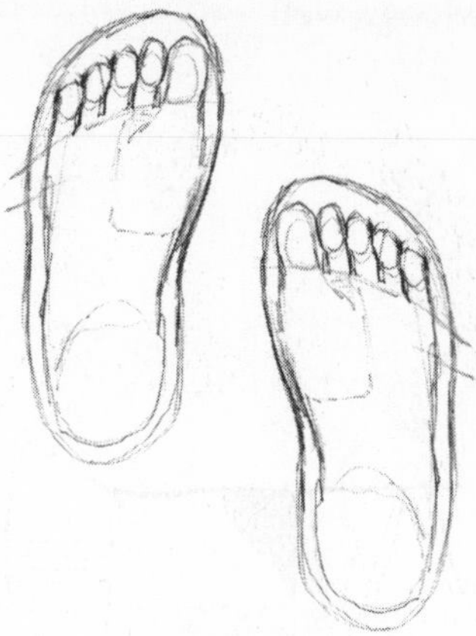

Shape
is everything
to drawing
correct shoes
-- even soles.

Here's another
cutaway portion
to examine.

Feet can also be used as tools for expression. Of course, there are only rare instances of this, but nonetheless, when the situation calls for it, it is always good to have the knowledge well at hand.

PRACTICE PAGE

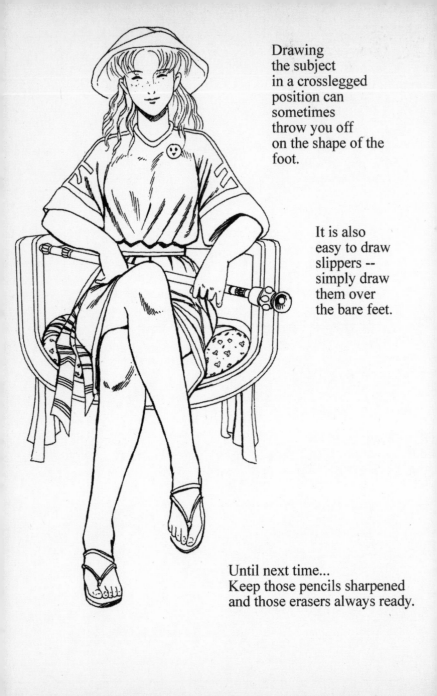

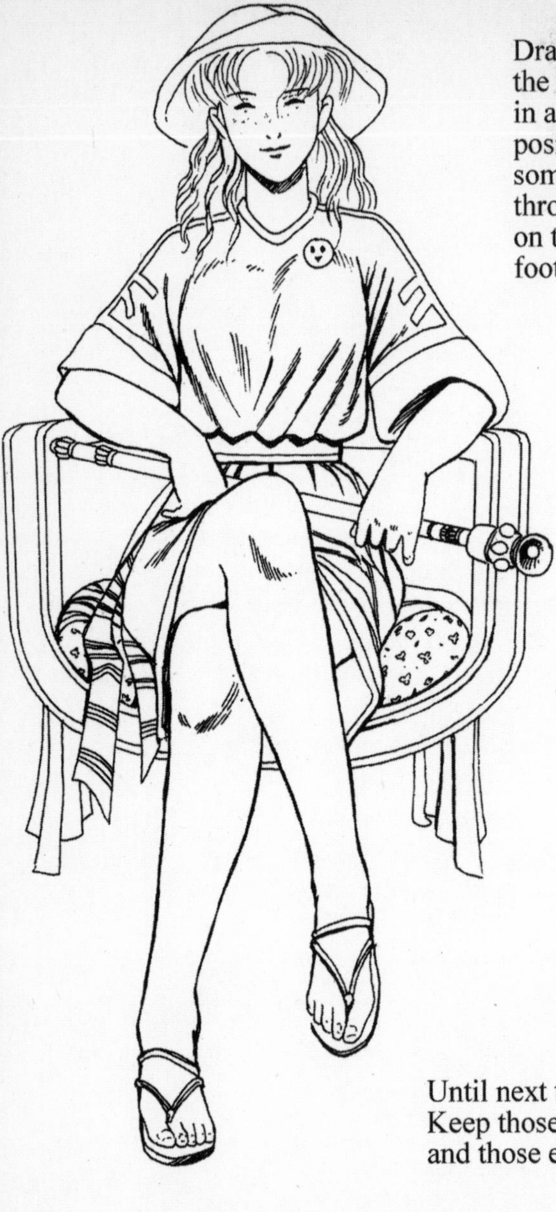

Drawing
the subject
in a crosslegged
position can
sometimes
throw you off
on the shape of the
foot.

It is also
easy to draw
slippers --
simply draw
them over
the bare feet.

Until next time...
Keep those pencils sharpened
and those erasers always ready.